1996

(Book 1 in the
90s Flashback Series)

KIRSTY MCMANUS

To the graduating class of Good Shepherd, 1997

THANKS TO...

I know I've said this before, but I am so lucky to have an amazing group of people in my life who are willing to take the time to read my stuff and give encouraging feedback.

Thank you, Diane. You are consistently helpful and always know exactly what to say (not just in terms of my books, either!). I value our friendship very much.

Thank you, Sofie. Sometimes I think you're too nice. Be harsher!

Thank you, Natasha! You gave me the kick-start I needed in order to take this book seriously!

Thank you, Louise. I love that you give me a slightly different perspective. It makes my work stronger.

Thank you, Anna! For this book in particular, it was great to get an 'insider's' opinion to make sure I was being authentic to the time and place.

And a super big thank you to Lindsay. You are an awesome editor and I look forward to working with you again!

ONE

Saturday 22nd June 1996

Dear Diary,

What a crappy day! I mean, it started out OK, but it ended pretty badly. I stayed at Kelsey's last night and we slept in until lunchtime, so that was all right. But then I got home, and Mum was all mad because I hadn't done enough around the house or something…she has no idea how busy my life is! Between school, work, dealing with girl dramas, and managing my love life, I don't really have any time left over to worry about stupid things like whether I've left my clothes on the floor in my bedroom. Does it really matter in the scheme of things?

Anyway, I had to work from 4 – 8 tonight and then Kelsey and I went to Rachel's party. That's when things took a turn for the worse…

"Anna! Are you still reading that damn diary?"

I look up at Ed, surprised by his tone. "What do you mean? I only found it this morning."

"Yes, but you've been glued to it for the last hour and a half. It's like you're obsessed or something."

"That's a bit harsh. I wouldn't say I was *obsessed*. Just interested in what I got up to back in high school."

He wrinkles his nose. "High school was bad enough the first time around. I couldn't think of anything worse than reliving it."

1

"But that's the interesting thing. I thought high school was awful, too. I was always stressed out…I was insecure…and I never knew who my real friends were—but reading back now I can see it wasn't all bad." I close the diary and stand up to give my husband a hug. "But don't think for a second I wish I were anywhere else right now."

He half-heartedly returns the embrace. "Okay, sorry I hassled you. But what was I supposed to think? You've had this dopey grin on your face all morning. And look!" He points to the words I LOVE JOHN written on the spine of the diary.

I frown. "I don't understand why you'd be annoyed by that. I don't even know which John that was."

"Well, that's not very comforting. How many Johns were you in love with?"

"It's not as bad as it sounds. Mostly celebrity ones, like Travolta. And Depp. Although, I probably would have written Johnny if that was the case…"

"Stop! I get it. You were a little groupie."

I stare at him. "Why does this bother you so much?"

"I don't know. It just doesn't seem healthy."

"Are you annoyed because you're not mentioned in there?"

"Don't be silly. We hadn't even met."

I squeeze his cheeks, trying to lighten the mood. "Aw, my poor little baby is jealous."

He slaps my hands away. "I'm not jealous. Forget it. Do whatever you want to do. I have to go, or I'll be late."

Wow. Okay. He is genuinely affected by this. "Do you think you'll be out all day?" I ask in a small voice.

"I don't know yet. I'll text you later."

"All right. And I'll put the diary away. I'm sorry if I made you feel weird."

He gives me a peck on the cheek. "I'll see you this afternoon."

I watch him leave, feeling a strange mix of emotions. I'm not obsessed with the past, am I? It wasn't like I was gushing about all the people I used to be friends with, or all the boys I had crushes on. I really did not know who the John was on the spine, because I didn't date one in 1996. And it's not like I had started today determined to relive my so-called 'glory days.' I had needed some inspiration for a new blog recipe and had gone to the garage to locate my old cookbooks. My parents recently downsized their house, and Dad had dropped off a box containing my diaries and some other stuff a few months back. I forgot it was even there until this morning when I stumbled upon it by accident.

It's so strange, reading back over your life as an adult. The events are familiar, but it's like they happened to someone else. And I was so clueless! Reading between the lines now, I can see how things really were. For example, I always thought of myself as a bit of a loner, but looking back, I was constantly surrounded by people. And I clearly didn't appreciate how much my poor parents suffered with me flitting in and out at all hours, not considering their situation for even a second.

I carry my diary into the garage and tuck it back in the box. There are at least half a dozen other diaries in there, mixed in with some old CDs, stuffed toys, and junk jewellery. I don't have anything pressing to do today, but Ed's reaction just now has made me feel strangely guilty. Further exploration can wait until later.

I go back inside and straighten the house. Not that it needs a lot of tidying. Ed and I are both very house-proud, so we always put everything away as soon as we've used it. We live in a restored Queenslander in Balmoral—a three-bedroom home with newly painted eggshell walls and blonde timber floorboards. Sometimes I wander down the hallway and marvel over the fact that I co-own this place with my handsome husband. We've both worked very hard to get where we are—Ed is a criminal defence lawyer at a well-known firm on Eagle Street—and I've made a bit of a name for myself as a food blogger. Today is Saturday, but lately Ed has been working on the weekends to try and clear a backlog of cases, so I've been treating Saturday as a workday, too.

After making the bed and loading the breakfast dishes into the dishwasher, I head into my study to boot up my computer. I run a healthy dessert website, and I am very fortunate to be paid for doing something I love. I got into the business before every man and his dog decided to do the same thing, so I already had all my processes refined, plus a loyal fan base by the time the internet got crowded. I have also published a cookbook, which brings in some passive income, and I have an ongoing sponsorship with a nutritional supplement company. They basically pay me to advertise their products and incorporate their ingredients into my recipes. I have over four hundred thousand Instagram followers, and my blog gets a couple of million visits each month.

Before I started doing this, I studied to be a pastry chef at a school in Paris, and then I did a dietician's course when I returned to Australia. These days, I try and stay up to date with workshops and online study.

But my day begins fairly boringly with admin. I quickly skim through my emails and find the usual…a ton of spam and businesses wanting me to promote their overpriced detox diets and exercise programs. I don't even reply to them anymore. I have an exclusive deal with my sponsor, and I only agreed to work with them because I believe in their products.

After approving a few dozen reader comments on my blog, I open up Wordpress to type up my next recipe. I already tested it out yesterday: a date and walnut slice made with almond meal and coconut flour.

I spend a bit of time creating a cute backstory—today's being inspired by the past and recalling my grandmother's fantastic baking from when I was a child. She was an amazing cook, even up to the day she died. I learned a lot from her.

I include all the ingredients and method for my latest creation, and then upload the photos I've already taken. Fortunately, this batch didn't need much Photoshopping. I'm quite proud of my food photography. It took a bit of practice, but I noticed that my following increased once I figured out the best angles and lighting for my dishes.

After reading over everything a couple of times to check for errors, I click *Publish*. I then post to Twitter, Instagram, and Facebook, letting everyone know that a new recipe is up.

There.

I then remember I wanted to do something nice for Mum. I spoke to her last night on the phone, and she's going through a bit of a rough patch. I navigate to a florist website that delivers to her area and pick out a brightly coloured bouquet of gerberas. In the accompanying message I say I hope she's feeling a bit better and that I'll visit her soon.

I sit back and rest my arms behind my head.

What now? I was supposed to plan a few recipes for next week, which is why I was in the garage earlier looking for inspiration, but I don't really feel like doing that now. I could go to the gym, but it's pouring rain outside, and I don't want to get wet.

I think back to Ed's earlier behaviour. Surely his reaction was a bit over the top? My husband is usually oblivious to what I do in the mornings because he's busy getting ready for work. I've learned to give him his space so he can read the news and eat his breakfast in peace. The only time we really exchange words is when I give him his morning coffee, and even then, it's mostly just me asking if he's got a big day ahead. He explained to me once that he has a particular set of thought processes that allow him to mentally prepare for the demands of his job, and any external distractions can have severe negative consequences for his clients.

The last thing I want to do is inadvertently contribute to one of Ed's clients going to jail, so I always try and save any news I want to talk about until after he gets home in the evening.

Anyway, my point is, to have him be *that* affected by me flicking through an ancient high school diary is kind of strange.

There's a knock at the door, happily giving me something else to focus on. I pad down the hall and collect a small box lying on my front step. The delivery guy has already disappeared. Weird. I don't remember ever getting a delivery on a Saturday before.

I carry it through to the dining room, tear off the packing tape, and peek inside. It looks like my latest bunch of supplements have arrived.

I pull out the containers, one by one, and place them on the dining table.

The first is greens powder. I could probably put that in my next smoothie recipe. The second and third jars are flavoured protein. I could maybe put them in an energy ball or slice.

The last jar is much smaller than the others. I hold it up and read the label.

YOUTH COMPOUND – Wind back the years with our revolutionary formula.
Feel instantly energised!
Dosage: Half a teaspoon dissolved in room temperature water. Effects will last for
approximately twelve hours.
30 doses.

Twelve hours? Is that all? Is it supposed to have some sort of cumulative effect over time or something? I open the jar and smell the contents. It has a faint chlorine scent and looks like salt crystals. I shrug and go to the sink to fill a glass with water, sprinkling a few of the crystals on top.

The water bubbles and turns purple. I wait until it has fully dissolved before taking a sip.

Yuck! It's a good thing I trust this company's products. It's like drinking poison! If they want me to advertise this for them, they're going to have to work on the taste.

I down the rest in one gulp and wince. Maybe next time, I could disguise the flavour with some juice or sweetener.

I wonder how I'll know if it's working. Will it be like a caffeine rush? Or an alcohol buzz?

I might have a shower while I wait. I don't want to be too distracted if the effects are only subtle. I walk towards the bedroom, starting to undress along the way, but before I even get there, I feel woozy. Wow. This stuff is strong.

I unsteadily make my way to the bed and plonk down on the edge, flopping backwards and staring at the ceiling. My vision swirls. I hope I haven't overdosed. Maybe I should call an ambulance.

The spinning gets faster. And faster.

Then everything goes black.

TWO

I open my eyes, feeling disoriented. That stuff really knocked me about. The room is still spinning, and I can't make my eyes focus.

After a moment, I sit up and take a few deep breaths.

But something isn't quite right.

This isn't my room. Or my house. Although, as my brain catches up, I realise I know this place.

I'm at Kelsey's. As in my high school best friend Kelsey who I haven't spoken to in almost twenty years. And I'm in Shell Beach. More than an hour and a half's drive from Brisbane. What on earth? I groggily look around at the movie posters on the wall—*Twister, Trainspotting,* and *Billy Madison*...the CDs strewn on the carpet beside the bed—Alanis Morisette's *Jagged Little Pill,* Red Hot Chili Peppers' *One Hot Minute,* and Garbage's self-titled album...and then at the body lying asleep beside me in the satin-sheeted bed.

I scream.

Kelsey grabs her pillow and covers her head.

"What is wrong with you?" she moans. "It's still the middle of the night."

I lift up the edge of the pillow and then drop it again. It's as if I've been burned.

"You're...you're so young!"

"Can we please do this later?" her muffled voice complains.

I push myself away from her and roll off the side of the bed. After stumbling to my feet, I launch myself at the mirror mounted on the side of her wardrobe.

"Holy shit."

"For heaven's sake, Anna. What is wrong with you?"

"I'm…am I sixteen?"

Kelsey finally emerges from under her pillow. "Not for much longer. Are you going through some sort of early-life crisis or something? Has this got something to do with Todd?"

I stroke the skin on my cheek and under my eyes, ignoring Kelsey's question. It's so smooth! And then I look down at my body, currently clad in a tiny peach-coloured silk slip.

"Oh my God! I look amazing!"

"You're freaking me out, babe."

"I'm freaking myself out! What date is it?"

"I don't know. Sometime in June."

"And the year?" I need to hear her say it.

"Are you serious?"

"Yep."

"1996. Did you have a nightmare or something? Are you still drunk? I knew I should have stopped you doing those tequila shots last night. You didn't swallow the worm, did you?"

"We drank tequila?"

"*You* did. I only had wine. Don't you remember? Ellie came over and we were playing that stupid drinking game."

Ellie? Wow, that's a name I haven't heard for a while. Kelsey and I were kind of friends with her, but she only seemed to make time for us when the more popular girls were ignoring her.

9

"Uh, right."

"You were a mess. I'm surprised you're not puking your guts up right now."

I mentally probe my body. Apart from a tiny headache, I feel surprisingly good. Better than I have in ages.

"I actually feel pretty awesome!"

"Great. Now can we go back to sleep? In case you've forgotten, we didn't get to bed until a few hours ago."

"I'm too excited to sleep!"

Kelsey pulls the pillow over her head again. "Go and annoy someone else, then. I'll be up after lunch."

I giggle. This is insane! Am I really somehow back in 1996? What the hell was in that Youth Compound?

Wait. I need to stop and think about this logically for a second. There are only a few explanations that can make sense here:

1. The Youth Compound contains some sort of hallucinogenic drug and I'm basically tripping.

2. I was tired after a morning of dealing with Ed's weird mood, and the Youth Compound contained a sedative that put me to sleep—in which case I am having a very lucid dream.

3. The Youth Compound is a vitamin form of a DeLorean, and I've travelled back in time, *Back to the Future* style.

I don't *really* think it could be that third one, but I'm not going to completely discount it until I have more information.

Whatever the reality, it's pretty impressive that my brain can conjure this all up from over twenty years ago. I'd forgotten the ratty shagpile carpet on the floor and exposed brick on the walls.

I venture into the hall and down the stairs. The TV is on in the living room, and Kelsey's older brother Andy is watching *Ren and Stimpy*. I freeze.

The last thing I want to do is talk to Andy—even in a hallucinogenic dream. I never liked him in the nineties, and knowing what happens in the future, I was definitely right to feel that way.

I start to creep away, but he spots me. He smiles a greasy smile.

"Anna. Are you trying to hide from me?"

I shiver and quickly cover my chest with my arms. I wish I were wearing something a little more conservative.

"I was just…uh…going to have a shower," I improvise. Even though the shower is upstairs.

He jumps up and plants himself in front of me quicker than I thought possible. "Would you like some company?" he purrs.

I slowly back up the stairs. "No, thank you."

"Are you sure?"

I try not to shudder too obviously. He has lank, shoulder-length hair and bloodshot eyes. He reeks of body odour, cigarette smoke, and rum. I focus on the Metallica shirt underneath the red flannel he's wearing. It has a skeleton playing guitar on it, and the skeleton looks like Slash from Guns n Roses. Weird.

"You wondering what's under here?" he asks, pulling the side of his shirt up and revealing a skinny white stomach.

I almost laugh. Seriously?

He catches my smirk, and it seems to annoy him. "What's so funny, princess?"

"Nothing." I decide it wouldn't be wise to taunt him, considering what I know he's capable of.

He runs a nicotine-stained finger down my cheek. "You better shower quickly, sweetheart. I need to use the bathroom soon, as well, and I won't wait politely at the door if you're in there too long."

Well, I'm definitely not going to wash here now.

"Duly noted," I say, turning and trying to escape.

He grabs my arm, and I flinch. It's okay. This isn't real. His eyes travel up and down my body as if he has x-ray vision.

After a moment, he seems to get bored.

"Nah. You're too flat-chested for me." He slouches off back to the TV.

I turn and hurry upstairs, quickly changing into my day clothes—which happen to be a pair of Tencel jeans and a midriff-baring top. Did I not own anything that covered a reasonable proportion of my body? I then shove all my other stuff into my bag. Kelsey is dead to the world again, so I scribble her a note and leave it on her bedside table.

I toss my bag over my shoulder and head back downstairs to the front door. Thankfully, Andy doesn't hassle me further.

Out on the street, I pause to consider my next move. I'm going to assume for now that I'm not physically moving around in the real world, and that I'm still just lying on my bed in Brisbane. I really don't want to end up like those poor people who take PCP and launch themselves off cliffs, thinking they can fly.

Would I have driven here? Assuming I'm playing by 1996 rules and it's June, it's still three months until I turn seventeen—so I almost certainly wasn't driving independently. I look up and down the street to see if I recognise any cars, just in case, but I don't. I learned to drive in my mum's Mazda 121—what we used to call the bubble car.

If none of this is real, I should just be able to steal a car, shouldn't I? But I can't quite bring myself to do it. Kelsey's mum's car isn't in their carport, and the idea of smashing someone else's window seems a bit violent. Besides, it's not like I know how to hotwire a vehicle.

I sigh. It looks like I'll be walking or catching public transport home. Home.

Home in 1996 is here in Shell Beach, and about a ten-minute drive from where I'm currently standing.

I don't really want to walk, though. Maybe I'll call a cab. I open my bag and rummage around for my mobile.

Good grief. Was my phone really this huge? I pull out a massive block from the depths of my luggage and stare at the handset. It weighs a ton.

What was the cab number again?

And then I realise I should probably check whether I have enough money for a cab. Going through my purse, I find two twenty-dollar notes and a handful of change. How much would a taxi cost? Surely not more than twenty. But then, will I be leaving myself short later? This is all too hard.

I shove the phone back in my bag and see a public transport timetable folded up in there. It says a bus should be along in a few minutes. Okay. That might be the safer option.

I head over to the bus shelter and wait. The surrounding houses look so new! I haven't been back to this street for more than five years in my real life, but I remember feeling a little depressed when I saw how run-down all the buildings were last time I passed through.

The bus arrives and I jump on, handing the driver some coins. I hope it's enough. He gives me a strange look and hands nearly all of them back.

Ha-ha. Whoops.

I gaze out the window at my old neighbourhood and wonder if I could do anything I wanted. Could I fly? Or run super-fast? I figure I can experiment later. Not that I'm going to hurl myself off a building or anything. We pass the supermarket that looks like it's only just had its grand opening…and the dozens of holiday apartment buildings all painted in shades of salmon and burnt yellow. In the future, they're all white. Personally, I like the salmon and burnt yellow. They seem less sterile somehow.

We pass a street that is barely populated apart from a service station. Wow. In just over twenty years, this place will be heaving with the trendy paleo crowd and weekend cyclists.

My bus pulls up at the entrance to my housing estate, and I hop off. I start the walk I did countless times as a teenager, but which I haven't done since I graduated high school.

Making sure no one is watching, I leap into the air and flap my arms, just in case I have special dream superpowers. I only succeed in tripping over and skinning my knee. The pain feels very much real. Interesting.

When I reach my front yard, I almost burst into tears. It doesn't look wholly different to how it is in the future, only my parents don't live here anymore. They're now in an apartment in Noosaville that doesn't even exist in 1996.

I go inside, but I don't see anyone right away, so I head to my bedroom to do some research.

Oh, my bedroom! How I've missed you! My parents wasted no time converting this space into a guest room once I moved out after high school. My eyes suck in all the details: the pine dresser with mirror on top…all my makeup and jewellery…my midnight-blue bed covers with the gold moons and suns printed on them…the matching lamp…and of course, the oversized stereo on the floor in the corner that can play both cassettes and CDs.

I hurry over to my bedside drawer and pull out my diary. I open up to the last entry and see it's the day before the one I was reading this morning. Which means today is Saturday the twenty-second of June, the same date as the future.

I quickly skim through the pages I read this morning to re-confirm a few details. Ah, that's right. I'm in my second last year of school and I have my learner's licence, but I can only drive Mum's car if she or Dad are with me. I work at the local video store, and I'm currently dating Todd.

Oh no. Todd.

There's a knock on my door. "Anna? Can I come in?"

I freeze. Mum.

I quickly shove the diary back in the bedside drawer and casually open my bedroom door.

I should have been prepared, but I'm not. The tears that were threatening to spill when I was outside now run free. I lean forward and envelop my very young-looking mother in a bear hug. She can't be much older than I am now.

She seems taken aback. "Are you okay, honey? What's wrong?"

"Nothing," I sob. "It's just so good to see you."

She laughs. "You only saw me last night. What's all this about?"

I don't say anything, continuing to embrace her and bawling like a baby. She looks so good. The last twenty-plus years have not been kind to her. Her and Dad have gone through a lot.

Mum gently extricates herself from my grasp. "Are you sure you're okay?"

I nod.

"I was just coming to get your washing. Do you want to add anything from your bag?" she asks.

"Oh, no, that's fine. I'll do it later."

My mother looks at me strangely. "Since when do you do your own laundry?"

"I just want to help. I'd be happy to do everyone's," I offer.

"You'll do *everyone's* washing? Sweetie, you haven't hit your head or anything, have you?"

"No! Why don't you go and relax? I'll sort out everything soon."

Mum shakes her head. "Okaaayyy…"

She goes to leave and then stops. "I'm heading to The Palace in an hour or so. Did you want to come?"

"Uh, sure."

"Great."

Mum walks off, muttering to herself. I think I've weirded her out.

I have time for a shower before we leave, so I head to the bathroom and strip down. It doesn't feel right to ogle my teenage body, so I avert my eyes and step into the shower to wash my hair. My crazy, frizzy, pre-coloured hair. The scent of the Revlon Flex shampoo on the shower rack triggers off a whole new set of feelings. So does my Body Shop strawberry bath wash. I once read that out of all of the senses, smell is most closely linked to memory. I can definitely vouch for that.

After rinsing, I step out and wrap myself in a towel. After marvelling at my face in the mirror for a moment, I decide that my appearance would be greatly improved by a little eyebrow maintenance. I can't believe my mum used to let me out of the house with them looking the way they do!

I quickly shape the two caterpillars perched above my eyes, being sure not to pluck them too thin, but making them look a million times better than before. I inspect the result. I can see traces of the older me in there. The dark green eyes…the nose with the slight curve in it…the freckles on my cheeks.

I look in the cabinet for my hair dryer and straightener.

The dryer is easy enough to find, but the straightener? Where on earth is my straightener?

Is that it? I reach into the back and pull out what I assumed was the straightener but is actually a crimper.

Oh no. Now I remember. Straighteners didn't properly exist in the mid-nineties. At least not for the general public to purchase.

I blow-dry my frizz into submission and then drag the crimper through it in a continuous motion, remembering that this is what I actually did to smooth out my locks back in 1996.

I then change back into my clothes. I can't seem to find anything that covers my belly, but I suppose when you're sixteen and have a flat stomach, there's no reason not to flaunt it.

After a quick spritz of CK One, I head downstairs.

I can't wait to see what happens next.

***

When I reach the ground floor, I hear noise coming from the living room. I head in that direction and see my sister Amy sitting on the floor, watching what looks like the Top 40 on Rage.

If I had been shocked at how young my mum looked, I am absolutely blown away by twelve-year-old Amy. She couldn't possibly ever have been that sweet-looking, could she? The Amy I know now is a tattoo-covered hipster living in New Farm. We're not very close, because she thinks I'm too conservative.

"Hey," I venture cautiously.

She looks up. "Oh, hey." She stares at me. "What have you done to yourself?"

For a second, I wonder what she's talking about. And then she points to my eyebrows.

"Oh, um, just a bit of grooming."

"They look good."

"Thanks."

"You're home early."

"Am I? I guess I couldn't sleep. And then Kelsey's brother was being weird."

Amy wrinkles her nose. "That Andy totally creeps me out."

17

I'm not sure I ever had this conversation with Amy in the real 1996. "Has he ever done anything to you?"

"No, but it's the way he looks at me. I don't trust him."

"You shouldn't. Make sure you're never alone with him."

"Don't worry. We will *never* be alone together."

In the future, Andy is caught with a bunch of drugs and suspected of spiking women's drinks with Rohypnol before presumably taking advantage of them. I don't know all the details, because Kelsey and I had stopped hanging out before he was arrested.

I look over at the TV. Shaggy's *Boombastic* is playing.

"I haven't heard this song in ages!" I say excitedly.

"What are you talking about? You play it on repeat. I'm sure I heard you listening to it yesterday."

"Oh, I guess it just seems like ages," I bluff.

"You're so weird." Amy looks back at the screen.

I hear someone come up behind me, and I turn just in time to see Dad leaning in to give me a kiss on the cheek. "Hey, sweetie."

Again, I should have been ready for it, but Dad's younger appearance also catches me off-guard. He has a lot more hair in 1996, and his eyes are brighter.

"Hi, Dad."

"What's going on here?" He draws a circle in the air around my face.

"Nothing."

"I like how you normally look," he grumbles.

"I think she looks great," Amy defends me.

I shoot her a grateful smile.

Mum appears in the living room. "Ready to go?" she asks me.

"Yep."

She directs her attention to Amy. "Are you sure you don't want to come, too?"

"No, thanks. I want to make a mix tape to take to Sam's later." I note the piece of paper beside her. We both used to write down all the songs in the Top 40 and then work out which ones were cassette-worthy. I experience a pang of nostalgia. Sure, we now have Spotify and YouTube, but there was something special about waiting the whole week for the Top 40 show on Saturday morning and taping your favourite tunes.

"We won't be long," Mum tells Dad. "You're working at four, aren't you?" she asks me.

I have no idea. "Uh, I think so?"

"We'll make sure we're back by three."

Dad waves us off. Amy is already watching the next song. Ugh. *The Macarena*. I don't miss that at all.

"Oh, I should put the washing on before we go," I say, remembering my promise.

Mum laughs. "It's okay, honey. I'll do it when we get home. But thanks for the offer. I appreciate that you even thought to suggest it."

I follow her out to the garage.

You know what? I'm quite looking forward to spending the day with my mum. I hardly ever get to do this anymore.

THREE

My heart swells at the sight of our old Toyota Tarago. My parents must have had a taste for bubble-shaped vehicles in the nineties.

I jump into the passenger side. Mum gets in the driver's seat and reverses out onto the road. Just like in the future, she has the radio tuned to easy listening. A song by the Fine Young Cannibals is playing, and I smile sadly, watching her bounce around to the beat. It's been a long time since I saw her with this much energy.

In 2001, Mum developed chronic fatigue syndrome. For several years, she struggled to even get out of bed and do basic things like brush her teeth and shower. She spent a ton of money on specialists, but no one could give her a diagnosis. Some doctors even told her it was psychological, and she just needed to snap out of it. Or they told her she needed to follow an exhausting exercise regime that just made her feel worse.

It wasn't until a couple of years ago that she found someone who had experience with the condition and called it by its official name: myalgic encephalomyelitis, or ME. The problem is, they still don't really know what causes it, and everyone has different symptoms, so Mum is always trying different things in the hope that a magic combination will finally cure her.

Since developing it, she's had periods of time where she almost seems normal, but then she'll relapse again. This year seems to have been particularly hard on her. Whenever I call and visit, she can barely muster the energy to talk. It's been really tough on Dad, too. He had to take a demotion at work so he could spend more time looking after Mum on her bad days. And now that they're both nearing retirement they don't have a lot of money. I think their final years are going to be difficult if Amy and I don't chip in financially. At least they have somewhere to live, and they've been able to save the profit from the sale of our family home.

I study the woman sitting next to me now. She was so cool in the nineties! I even like her clothes. Today she's wearing a black-and-gold paisley dress with spaghetti straps and a black cardigan. She even has on black knee-high boots. How did I not covet her wardrobe?

"You look great, Mum," I say.

She stops bouncing. "Who are you and what have you done with my daughter?"

"I'm serious. I really like your dress. And those boots."

"Why, thank you."

We drive in silence the rest of the way to The Palace Mall. The highway mustn't have been completed for another couple of years because we're on the less direct coast road. And while it's at least ten minutes longer, I always preferred it anyway, catching glimpses of the ocean through the trees. Today, the water is clear and flat. Of course, it's the middle of winter, so it would also be very cold.

The Palace is much smaller in 1996 than it is in the future. They've done at least two expansions between now and then. (Or is it then and now? I'm so confused.) Mum and I park in the undercover carpark and go inside. We pass the food court, which still contains the same kebab stall and Chinese food buffet as it does in the future, and head towards Target.

Just as we near the store's entry, someone calls out to Mum. We both turn and see a woman hurrying towards us. Oh no. It's Mary, a woman who Mum met through an art class, and who was the biggest gossip in town. That's one person I haven't missed seeing recently.

"Hey, girls!" She beams at us both. "How are you?"

Mum smiles her professional hostess smile—the one she used to reserve for people she didn't particularly like. "Not bad. What about you?"

"Oh, I'm good. Just buying a few bits and pieces." She zones in on Mum. "Eve, I've been meaning to catch up with you so I could tell you what happened with Wendy the other day."

Mum shoots me an apologetic look.

"I'm actually just out with Anna at the moment. We're having a bit of a mother-daughter morning…"

"Why don't the two of you join me for a cup of tea? Anna would be fine with that, wouldn't you, hon?"

"Well…"

"Anna has an appointment at the beautician in a few minutes," Mum cuts in. She looks at me pointedly. "Why don't you meet me back here in an hour?"

"Uh, okay. Yeah. Thanks."

Poor Mum. She's always been too nice for her own good. I'll owe her for sacrificing herself so I could be free. Which is a strange thought, considering this is probably all just a hallucination.

I pretend to walk to the beauty salon, checking to make sure Mary isn't looking before I hurry off in the other direction. I can't risk staying in this part of the mall in case I'm seen, so I head outside to a strip of older shops across the street. None of them are there in the future—it's a fancy food market now. I feel a pang of nostalgia as I pass the old piercing shop where I had my bellybutton done. Oh! And there's that cool alternative record store I used to visit with my friends. I was always too intimidated to go inside on my own.

I miss proper music stores. I know there are still a few around that sell DVDs and computer games alongside the latest Michael Bublé release, but they're not quite the same.

I go inside and inhale the musty scent of second-hand albums. I flick through the shelves, thinking about music in the nineties. Pearl Jam, Nirvana, Smashing Pumpkins…I just can't get excited about popular music anymore. Back in 1996, I used to wait for months for a new album to come out, and then I'd have to visit every shop in town to obtain that elusive copy or wait until it could be ordered in especially.

I wonder what the people of 1996 would think if I told them about Spotify? Or Shazam? I still find it amazing that my phone can tell me what song is playing nearby just by pressing a button.

I chuckle to myself while contemplating whether to buy a Rage Against the Machine album just for the fun of it.

"Hi, can I help you there?"

I look up, and into the amused eyes of a grunge god. Wearing a name badge that says Kurt. Ha. It's like he was specifically made for this place.

I've always had a soft spot for long-haired boys who look like they stay up all night playing guitar and drinking scotch on the rocks. Which makes me wonder why I didn't end up with one. Actually, I know the reason. Guys like that make terrible long-term boyfriends, often being unemployed and depressed artistic types.

"Sorry, I was just thinking about technology."

"In what way?" He appears to be genuinely interested in my reply.

"I was just wondering whether CDs will stand the test of time." Of course, I know they're practically obsolete in just over twenty years, but I can't say that outright.

"Probably not. If vinyl and cassettes are anything to go by, I'm betting something else will come along in the future. And probably sooner, rather than later."

I nod. He's more than just a pretty face.

"Do you think it would be cool if they had tiny machines that held hundreds of digital songs? Or if you could store them on your mobile phone?"

He thinks for a second. "I guess it would be more convenient than carting around a crate of vinyl or a CD wallet. But I have to admit, I'm a bit of a purist. I love how vinyl sounds."

I smile. "Typical music store guy answer."

"But it *does* sound better! Way better than cassette. Although, CDs, I'm not sure about yet."

"I can't tell the difference," I admit.

"Typical philistine answer," he teases.

"I'm sorry if I don't live up to your musical snob standards," I sniff melodramatically.

"Here, let me show you." He ushers me towards a room behind the counter.

"Am I allowed back there?"

"Yes, because I'm in charge today."

"Okay, then." I follow him into a small room filled with floor-to-ceiling CDs and records. An old blanket-covered couch leans against one wall, and a record player rests beside it.

"Take a seat," he says, gesturing to the couch.

I cautiously sit down.

He shuffles amongst the shelves, looking for something.

"Is your name really Kurt?" I ask.

"Yes!" He turns around and stares at me for a second, feigning outrage. "Why? Do you think I've stolen Kurt Cobain's name for the extra cred?"

24

"It did cross my mind."

"I was actually named after Kurt Vonnegut. My parents were fans."

"Ah. *Slaughterhouse Five?*"

He raises an eyebrow. "You've read it?"

"Uh, yeah," I say cagily. I don't want to admit I only read it a few years ago in my early thirties and I wasn't a fan.

"I tried to read it and couldn't finish it. But then I'm not much of a reader," he says. "What did you think of it?"

"It was okay, but not my favourite," I confess.

"I don't blame you." He turns back to the shelves and keeps looking for something. I study his back. He has on a black T-shirt (naturally) with ripped jeans, rocking them like the cool cat he is. His hair is identical to Eddie Vedder's in his *Vitalogy* days, and I have to stop myself from reaching out and touching it. He's tall and thin and looks like he lives on cigarettes and alcohol. But who knows? He might just have a fast metabolism. He is also in his early-twenties, which is bordering on too old for sixteen-year-old me, and much too young for future me. Not that it matters, because I'm married. To an amazing, perfect man. And even if this isn't technically happening and Kurt is a figment of my imagination, I seem to have *some* control over my actions, so I should act accordingly.

There is definitely something about him, though. Like he's someone I should have known already.

He finally finds what he's looking for and slides a record out of its protective sleeve. He checks it for dust before gently placing it on the turntable.

I love how much care he takes with this little ritual. He's obviously performed it countless times before.

He crawls over and climbs onto the couch next to me and closes his eyes.

"Don't you think it sounds warmer somehow?" he asks.

"I'm not sure," I murmur. I strain my ears to hear the difference.

"This is Bob Dylan's *Sad-Eyed Lady of the Lowlands*. It sounds amazing on vinyl. Did you know he did this whole eleven-minute track in one take at the end of an eight-hour recording session?"

"Impressive."

I close my eyes, too, and open up my mind, allowing the music to flow through my brain. And then I get it. I've never been much of a Bob Dylan fan but sitting here in this dingy back room in a record store seems to be the perfect place to listen to this exact song.

If I were really in 1996, this guy sitting beside me would now be in his mid-forties. And most probably unemployed and balding.

But I'm not thinking about that right now. This moment is all I care about. This little slice of time that stands all on its own. If it turns out I am actually in a *Back to the Future* situation, I may have just changed the universe irrevocably.

"You look so serious," he says.

I open my eyes and face him. He's watching me intently.

"I'm just trying to hear the difference."

"And can you?"

"I think so."

"Hello?" a voice calls from the shop.

Kurt and I jump simultaneously.

"I better get that," he says, reluctantly standing up.

"Of course."

"You can stay and listen a bit longer if you like."

"Maybe just for a minute."

I watch him leave and try to relax into the music again, but it's no use. The spell has been broken.

I stay for another five minutes before sneaking out while Kurt is busy talking to a customer.

I'm out on the street when I hear him calling out.

"Hey! What's your name?"

I turn around. "Anna."

"You should come back another day and I'll show you more stuff that sounds good on vinyl."

"Maybe."

"I'm here on weekends and then Tuesdays and Wednesdays," he adds.

"Good to know."

He gives me a look that makes me think he's used to girls making more of an effort around him. "Bye, Anna."

"Bye, Kurt."

He shakes his head and goes back inside.

I don't stop smiling all the way back to The Palace.

***

Mum and I don't end up having afternoon tea together, because Mary took up all the available time.

"I'm so sorry, sweetie," Mum says as we drive back out to the main road. "Today didn't really go according to plan, huh?"

"It's all right. I had fun."

"Oh, good. So, you bought some new clothes?" She points to the two shopping bags at my feet. I couldn't resist. On the way back to meet Mum, I bought a pair of strappy sandals with a slight heel, and a form-fitting stripy dress with a slit up one side. I could never get away with a dress like that in the future.

"Yeah. How was your catch-up with Mary?"

Mum pulls a face. "Horrendous. I had to hear all the sordid details of poor Wendy's divorce. Honestly, I'm never telling that woman a single personal detail again. It would end up all over town within an hour."

"Lucky she doesn't have Facebook," I mutter.

"Sorry?"

"Oh, it's just lucky she doesn't have a way of spreading the information faster."

"Heaven forbid." She glances at me and then back at the road. "So, you're off to that party tonight?"

Party? Was I going to a party? I have a vague recollection of reading something to do with a party in my future diary before Ed interrupted me. Damn. I wish I'd had a chance to finish reading that entry.

"Uh, that's right."

"Is Todd going?"

"I think so. Why?"

"To be honest, I've never been a fan of that boy. He doesn't treat you well."

"Yeah, I agree." Todd was a tool. A very good-looking tool, but a tool, nonetheless.

Her face registers surprise. "Really? Then why are you dating him?"

"I don't know. We probably won't last much longer."

"Oh, okay. Is there anyone else you have your eye on?"

I blush. Which is a weird reaction, but I put it down to the fact that I can't tell her about Ed.

"Um, not really. I should probably just focus on school for a while."

Ha. Mum's going to think I've had a lobotomy or something.

Her mouth drops open. "Did I hear that correctly? Did you just say you wanted to concentrate on your schoolwork instead of boys?"

Oh God. I need to divert her attention so she doesn't start getting suspicious.

I look back at a shopping bag in the seat behind me. "I see you managed to squeeze in a bit of shopping, too."

"Yes. I went and bought a dress for your grandmother. Actually, thanks for reminding me. I almost missed the turn-off. I thought I'd quickly drop it off on the way home."

I freeze. "Grandma?" I say faintly.

"Is that all right?"

I almost hyperventilate. Grandma Millie died in 2003.

"Of course it's all right. I just didn't…never mind. I'm really looking forward to seeing her."

"You really are acting oddly today. You're not on drugs, are you?"

Possibly. Who knows what's going on?

"I'm not on drugs, Mum. I probably just didn't get enough sleep last night, that's all."

"Well, whose fault is that?"

"Mine. I know. Sorry."

We pull into the driveway of the retirement village where Grandma used to live and park near the front door.

"We can't stay for too long, because you'll be late for work," Mum says.

I follow her down a little path to a small villa with a pretty little garden. Grandma was always so proud of her roses.

I start to cry. I can't help it. This is all too much.

"Hello?" Mum calls through the screen door.

Grandma appears, exactly as I remember her. Her hair is completely white and cropped short. Her skin is all crepey, but she has sparkly, vibrant eyes.

"Oh, this is a lovely surprise!" she says, opening the door and ushering us in. She gives Mum a hug first and then looks at me.

"Are you okay, dear?" She leans in and wraps me up in her arms. I breathe in her lavender perfume and cry harder.

"For goodness sake, Anna. I don't know what's gotten into you today." Mum turns to Grandma. "Sorry, Mum. Anna's very up and down at the moment. I blame teenage hormones and lack of sleep."

"There's nothing wrong with a bit of emotion every now and again." She stands back and fixes her gaze on me. "You're fine, aren't you, darling?"

I nod, not quite able to speak yet.

"Good. Now let me get you a cup of tea."

"Oh, we can't stay long, I'm afraid," Mum says. "I just wanted to drop off a little something for you." She holds up the shopping bag.

"You shouldn't have." She takes the bag and peers inside before pulling out a floral sundress. "That's lovely, thank you. How much do I owe you?"

"Nothing. It's a gift."

"I do have money, you know."

"I never said you didn't, but I thought you could use a couple of new things. I know you probably won't be able to wear this outside right now without a coat, but when I saw it, I thought of you."

"Well, thank you, honey. That's very thoughtful of you. Do you at least have time for a snack? Or I can put a couple of pieces of my caramel slice in a container for you?"

"I would love some of your caramel slice," I answer for the two of us. I want to tell her how much she inspires my future career, how every time I bake, I feel closer to her. But I can't.

She beams. "Just a moment."

I look around her villa. The furniture is old, but it's well cared for. My grandmother had all her wits until the end, but she had bad knees and hips and often fell over. This retirement home allowed her to be mostly independent, but with back-up support close by. Grandpa Harry died in the early eighties, so she was on her own for a long time.

"Have you thought about what you want to do after you graduate next year?" Grandma asks me as she cuts up the slice.

"I was thinking of becoming a pastry chef," I tell her.

"This is the first I've heard of it," Mum says, bewildered. "I thought you wanted to be a dentist."

Oops. I'd totally forgotten that Mum and Dad tried to convince me to go into dentistry. I pretended to agree with them for a while, but I finally told them my true intentions just before I graduated.

"I think that sounds like an admirable choice," Grandma says. She hands me a container with the slice in it. I crack open the lid and inhale.

"I'll have to visit more often and get some practice with you."

She laughs. "Sweetheart, all women my age used to bake like this. We were basically forced to stay at home and look after the kids, and we had to do *something* once everyone went to school."

"Do you wish you'd been able to work outside the house?"

She shrugs. "I guess I never seriously thought about it. I just did what I had to do."

Mum starts walking towards the door, looking at her watch and then me. "We should probably get going."

I hand Mum the container of slice and then race over to give Grandma another hug. "I'm going to come back and visit again soon," I promise her. Obviously, if this is a hallucination that won't be possible, but it feels like the right thing to say.

"Anytime," she says.

Mum squeezes Grandma on the arm. "Have a great afternoon, Mum."

We head back out to the car and I climb into the passenger seat, barely paying attention to my surroundings. It didn't even occur to me that I could see Grandma here. Who else have I not visited since 1996 because they passed away? Or even just moved to a faraway location?

"What was all that about wanting to be a pastry chef?" Mum asks, still staring at the road. I look over and see she's trying hard to look casual.

"It was just an idea," I say lightly. "Nothing's set in stone." This might not be real, but I still don't feel like getting into an argument.

"Were you just saying it for your grandmother's sake? Or have you been promising your father and I dentistry for ours?"

"I'm considering them equally," I say firmly.

"You know dentistry will ensure financial security?"

"I do, Mum. And I promise I won't make any rash decisions."

"Good."

We're quiet for a few minutes.

I wonder if I could call in sick to work today. I say as much to Mum.

"If you're too sick to work, you're too sick to go to that party."

Do I even want to go to the party? Maybe I should just stay in tonight. Or I could sneak out. But our house isn't really designed for an easy escape. My bedroom is on the second floor and there aren't any trees or nearby walls for me to climb onto.

I don't really feel like working at a video store for the next four hours, but I suppose it's the only way I can guarantee my freedom later on.

The compromises you have to make as a teenager.

FOUR

Now this feels weird.

I walk through the door and into the video shop where I used to work. Paula, one of my old co-workers, is busy serving a long line of customers.

"I'm so glad you're here!" she cries, relieved. "It's crazy busy and Jill went home early because she started puking."

"Is she all right?" I ask, hurrying behind the counter and ushering some of the customers over to my side.

"I think she had alcohol poisoning," Paula says, rolling her eyes. "She's so selfish."

I laugh. I do remember Jill being a pretty big party animal. I'm surprised she ever showed up for work at all.

I look at the screen in front of me and feel a wave of relief. It's just like riding a bike. You never forget.

I scan the first customer's card and frown.

"I'm sorry, sir, but you have fifteen dollars owing on a new release you returned late a couple of weeks ago."

"But I brought it back the next day!" he protests.

"Uh…" I quickly read the notes on the customer's account, which suggests he's a repeat offender. "You might have to talk to the manager about that," I say apologetically. "You don't have to pay any off the fine tonight, but I don't have the authority to erase it."

He makes a hmphing sound but doesn't argue.

After he leaves, Paula laughs. "You go, girl. You do know that's the owner's daughter's new boyfriend, don't you?"

"Well, if he doesn't want to be charged any fines, he should use his girlfriend's account."

"Right on." She continues serving but keeps talking to me. "What did you get up to today? Please tell me it was something fun so I can live vicariously through you. I've been stuck inside on this gorgeous sunny day."

"Oh, I just went to The Palace with my mum."

And met a gorgeous boy who may not even exist.

"That's not quite what I envisioned. At least tell me you bought something nice?"

"I got a new dress and some shoes," I offer.

She laughs. "Eh, I guess that's better than nothing."

I look up at the next customer and do a double take.

"Todd!" I hadn't expected to see him out of context like this.

He looks at me through floppy brown hair with his intense dark eyes. "Hey, Anna."

"Are you renting a movie?"

"No," he says, vaguely annoyed. "I just wondered if I could talk to you for a minute."

I look at the line forming behind him and shrug awkwardly. "I have to serve these people, but I was going to see you at the party tonight anyway, wasn't I?"

He frowns. "Oh, right."

"Come find me when you arrive," I say, trying to appease him.

"Fine." He stalks off, muttering something that sounds like "can't even make some fucking time to talk to me…"

I look at Paula, and she nods her head in Todd's direction.

"Boys, huh?"

I smile. "Yeah."

I continue serving customers on autopilot.

I can't help entertaining the thought that this isn't actually a hallucination *or* a dream. It's a ridiculous concept, but what if I really *have* gone back in time? Do I want to stray too far from the original path? And where is sixteen-year-old Anna's mind right now?

The Youth Compound label said the effects were supposed to last for twelve hours. It's almost four-thirty now, so if I blacked out around ten this morning, it means I still have almost half my time left.

I figure I'll just avoid any dramatic decisions for the rest of the day. But then, what *is* a dramatic decision? I don't think I went to The Palace with Mum on this date last time. What if that was enough to mean I don't go to Paris after graduation? And what if I never meet Ed?

Panic rises in my chest. I'm paralysed with the possible fate of the world resting on my shoulders.

"Anna?"

Paula points to the line of impatient people standing in front of me.

"Hi, can I help you?" I say to the next customer.

The man smiles and approaches me. "Thanks, I'll take these." He pushes five adult movies towards me, his eyes glinting as if daring me to react.

Ew! He's got to be at least fifty. How can he be so brazen about his selection with a sixteen-year-old girl? At least, the appearance of one.

I snatch up his membership card and quickly scan the movies. I complete the rental in record time and plonk the cases down on the other side of the counter for him to collect. I turn to the next customer, ignoring the fifty-year-old.

It's going to be an interesting night.

***

Kelsey phones the shop at half past seven to invite me to her place before the party. "Do you want to get ready here and we'll split a cab?"

"Your brother isn't going to be there, is he?" I ask. I still feel icky about this morning.

"No. He's gone to Brisbane. He won't be back until tomorrow night. Why?"

"Oh, he was just being a bit weird this morning. Okay. I'll quickly go home and get my stuff after I leave here. I'll be at yours before eight thirty."

"Rad. See you soon."

I'm amazed at how easily I have slotted back into 1996. I feel like maybe I should be working out if I can wake up earlier or something, but I'm kind of enjoying myself. It's nice to have a break from reality, even if mine is usually pretty good.

After eight, I head home and pack a bag. Mum seems to feel sorry for me and offers to drive me to Kelsey's.

When we arrive, Mum kisses me on the cheek. "Be good. And let me know if you need me to pick you up later. I don't want you feeling stuck if you need to get away from Todd."

"I'll be fine. Thanks, Mum."

Kelsey is standing on the balcony on the second floor.

"Hurry up!" she calls. "I want to leave soon!"

I go inside, waving to Mum one last time before I head upstairs.

"Hey."

Kelsey is throwing items of clothing from her wardrobe onto her bed. "Hey."

"Can't decide what to wear?" I ask dryly.

"I was going to wear this." She holds up a tiny pink satin dress. "Only it has this weird stain on it. I'm not sure if it's wine or blood."

I inspect the stain near the neckline. "Why would it be blood?"

"I dunno. But I don't usually drink red wine. Either way, it's unwearable." She drops it on the floor and continues sifting through her wardrobe.

I open my bag and pull out my new dress and sandals.

"Oh, nice. They new?"

"Yep. I bought them today."

She looks at my face properly for the first time. "Hey, I like what you've done to your eyebrows. You look older."

I stifle a laugh. Only a sixteen-year-old would consider that a compliment.

"Thanks."

"So, are you all recovered after this morning? You still know what year it is?"

I'm actually surprised she remembered the conversation, considering she was half asleep then. "Uh, yeah. Sorry, I think I must have had a weird dream or something."

"That's cool. I once dreamt I went downstairs and found all these body parts, and I thought I'd murdered someone in my sleep. And then when I woke up for real, I was too scared to go and check whether everything was normal."

I laugh. This is nice. I'd forgotten how much fun I used to have with Kelsey. We had a falling out in 2000 and never reconnected, because she thought I slept with a guy she was dating. Obviously, I didn't, and he just told her we did to make her angry when she was trying to end their relationship. At the time, I was mad she believed him, but now whenever I think back, it just makes me sad.

37

I'm glad I get to hang out with her again today without any of that drama.

"I think you should wear the crushed velvet dress," I say, pointing to it on the bed.

"But it's so boring!"

"It's not. Wear it with your Docs and choker." Ha. I lived for nineties fashion.

"Okay," she sighs.

I never wore much makeup, so after putting on some mascara and swiping an orangey-red gloss over my lips, I watch Kelsey do her face. She was always really good at full makeup.

"So, what's happening with you and Todd?" she asks as she clamps an eyelash curler over the lashes on her left eye.

"Um, I don't know." I try to think back to when we broke up. Was it around this time? I know it was at some party, but I'm not sure if it was this one tonight.

"How can you not know? He's a total babe. What's the problem?"

"He's arrogant."

"I thought you liked arrogant."

Did I? I was a messed-up teenager.

"He just assumes I like everything he does."

Kelsey seems to have gotten bored of the conversation and stands back to check out her full reflection in the wardrobe mirror.

"I wonder if Aaron will be there tonight."

Aaron…Aaron…this is really stretching my memory now.

"Aaron?"

"Yeah. I know he's in year twelve, but he's friends with Rachel's brother, so maybe he'll drop by."

Oh. Aaron. He was the school captain. I never paid much attention to him, because he thought the year elevens were beneath him.

"Do you like him?" I ask.

She spins around and stares at me.

"Seriously? Have you been so wrapped up in your own world that you haven't listened to me tell you how much I love him for the last month?"

"Sorry. I'm having a really weird day."

"You can say that again."

She grabs her handbag and heads for downstairs. "You ready to go?"

"Yep."

I follow her out. I can't say I'm excited about this party, but I'm definitely intrigued.

FIVE

We arrive at Rachel's, and I experience my first sense of déjà vu all day. Everything else that happened earlier was either generic or new, so I didn't feel like I was living in *Groundhog Day* until now.

We walk up the driveway, which is brightly lit and contains several teenagers lounging on the pavement, passing around cigarettes. I want to lecture them about lung cancer and tell them that in the future they'll practically bankrupt themselves if they keep it up, but obviously I don't.

While I'm glad I've had the chance to reconnect with Kelsey, I'm not particularly excited to see everyone else. The novelty of being back in 1996 was fun for a few hours, but now that I'm here at this party, I'm having second thoughts.

Kelsey drags me through the front door and into Rachel's living room. Kids are dancing in the middle of the floor to Toni Braxton's *You're Making Me High*.

Why did I think this was a good idea? I should have just stayed home tonight.

"Oh my God! Look at Rachel and Scotty! I didn't even know they liked each other!"

I glance over and see them making out against the wall near the kitchen.

Oh, yeah. I remember this. This is definitely the night I broke up with Todd. Awesome.

Speak of the devil. Todd appears behind me and wraps his arms around my waist, nibbling my ear. "Hey, beautiful."

I jump back as if electrocuted. No one apart from Ed is allowed to touch me like that anymore. But of course, Todd still thinks I'm sixteen-year-old me. I try to make it look like I just stumbled.

"Hi, Todd." He's acting like he wasn't all moody when he saw me at work several hours ago. I can smell the Jim Beam on his breath, so maybe he's actually forgotten about it already.

"I'm going to see if Aaron is here," Kelsey tells me, skipping off.

Great. Now it's just me and Todd.

"How was your day?" I ask politely.

"Not bad. I hung out with the guys down the beach...smoked some weed...had a nap..."

"So, a pretty good day then?"

"Yeah, I guess it *was* a pretty good day." He looks around the room. "Oh, there's Paul. Paul! Over here!"

Paul, who I now remember was one of Todd's best friends, comes over.

"What's up?"

"Not much. Did you see the surf earlier? It looked so good. I would've taken my board with me, only the report on TV said it was going to be flat."

"Yeah, I managed to get a few waves in this afternoon. It was epic."

My eyes glaze over. I feel so out of place, standing here with two teenage boys talking about the surf. I notice a fully stocked bar nearby, with Rachel's brother standing guard. I slip away from Todd and Paul and go over.

What was his name again? Chris? Yeah, Chris.

"Are you in charge of the alcohol?" I ask.

He looks at me and smiles. "It seems that I am."

"Are you serving? Or making sure no one touches it?"

"A little of both. What are you after?"

"Anything that will help relieve the boredom of being here."

He laughs. "That bad, huh? Aren't you here with Lover Boy?" He tilts his head in Todd's direction.

"Unfortunately, yes."

His eyes light up. "Trouble in paradise?"

"Um, maybe. He doesn't know it yet, though."

"Well, in that case, you might need something strong. Let me make you a cocktail."

"Okay. Thanks."

I watch as Rachel's brother mixes up a drink with Southern Comfort, amaretto, juice, and a very large shot of gin.

"An Alabama Slammer," he says proudly, placing the drink in front of me.

I'm impressed and take a sip. "Hey, this is pretty good."

"I'm planning on working at a bar next year while I study at uni, so I thought I should get some practice in." He pulls a stern face. "You're over eighteen, right? Can I see some ID?"

I giggle, despite myself. Chris is funny.

I sip my drink and lean back against the wall beside the bar. "Thanks for this. I needed it."

"Are you going to break his heart tonight?" He nods at Todd again.

"Uh, I don't know." I don't really want a repeat of the scene from 1996 the first time around. That was ugly. But as long as I don't somehow end up alone with Todd in a bedroom, I should be fine. And if I can avoid him altogether, I might not have to deal with any awkwardness at all.

Chris sees my expression. "Are you okay? You know this is all just high school, right? Todd will get over it if you dump him.”

“I know. But I don't want to cause a scene.”

And then a vision of Biff Tannen married to Marty's mother flashes before my eyes. What if I'm in the real 1996 and by not breaking up with Todd tonight, I end up marrying him?

“Well, let me know if you get into a tight spot and I'll come rescue you. I'm going to escape this madness for a few minutes and grab some food. Hopefully, the bar won't be destroyed by the time I return.”

“Do you want me to watch it?”

“Nah, it's all right. You go have fun.”

“Okay. But if things get rowdy, I'll try and save the expensive booze.”

“Thanks.”

We share a conspiratorial look before he disappears.

Todd is instantly at my side. “You looked cosy just now.”

“What do you mean?”

“With Rachel's brother. What was going on there?”

“Nothing. He was making me a drink.”

“You weren't tuning him?”

Tuning him? Wow, I haven't heard that phrase in a long time.

“No, I was not *tuning* him.”

“You're being weird tonight. What's the matter?”

Remember that scene where Marty McFly was horrified by the fake boobs Biff made his mother get?

Nope. I can't risk it.

“You really want to know why?” I stare at him directly. “Because you never ask me anything about myself. You assume that I want to talk about your stupid day, where you got stoned and went surfing, but you don't actually stop to think about whether that is interesting to me. Newsflash, it's not! Have you ever thought to ask what *I* get up to on the days I don't see you?"

Clearly, I have some unresolved issues from this period of my life. And maybe, if I'm being really honest with myself, his behaviour is similar to how Ed treats me sometimes. I don't want to admit it, but now that I've made the connection, I can't un-make it.

He looks bewildered. "Have you got your period or something?"

I feel like I've been slapped. How dare this ridiculous little boy invalidate my feelings! I may not care about him now, but I really liked him back in 1996. At least this time, I'm more in control.

"Todd, you are immature, selfish, and arrogant. Our relationship is over."

His face registers surprise and then anger.

"Fucking slut," he hisses. "Fuck off, then. Go and fuck Chris because that's obviously what you were about to do anyway."

"For the record, I wasn't. But I certainly wasn't going to sleep with you either."

"Because you're an uptight virgin," he says louder than necessary. A few people look at me, but I don't care.

"I guess that makes you uptight, too," I say just as loud.

The same people snigger, and Todd's face goes red.

"Skank," he says as he storms off. I almost laugh. How can I be both promiscuous and virginal at the same time? I shouldn't have stooped to Todd's level, but he kind of deserved it. And knowing what he did to me in the original 1996 erases any trace of remorse I might have been feeling.

I down the rest of my cocktail and go back to the bar. Chris is nowhere to be found, so I pour myself half a glass of straight gin and swallow it in two seconds flat.

Uh…maybe I shouldn't have done that.

My head starts to spin, and I find it hard to focus. If I were paying attention, I would realise that this was the exact same feeling as this morning. But all I'm worried about is passing out in the middle of a party, especially if Todd is still around.

There doesn't seem to be anything I can do to stop it, though. I don't even think I can make it to the...

SIX

I peel one eye open. And then the other.

And audibly sigh in relief.

I'm back in my bedroom. The one I share with Ed in the future.

What a crazy dream!

Or was it?

I quickly roll over and notice that the other side of the bed is empty. For a second, I panic. What if everything that just happened was real and now Ed is no longer my husband?

Then I hear the shower.

Okay. So, I have someone else in my house who is familiar enough to bathe here. Of course it's Ed.

I tiptoe over to the closed door to the ensuite and slide it open.

Phew.

He's in there, soaping his chest. "Hey. How are you feeling?"

"Good. Great!" I have never been so relieved to see Ed in my entire life.

"When I got home last night, you were already out cold, asleep. I thought you must have been sick. You weren't even in your PJs."

"What time is it?"

"I don't know. Around seven, I guess? I have that golf thing today, so I'll have to leave soon."

I slept the entire day and night? Wow. So, I was having a dream that was basically in real time? Is that even a thing? How come I'm not starving or dying to use the bathroom?

I look at Ed closely. I feel like I'm only seeing him for the first time.

"I missed you," I say softly.

"I missed you, too," he says, although if I'm being picky, he doesn't sound like he really means it. Granted, he hasn't just experienced what I have.

"Do you mind if I join you?" I ask. I feel like the only way I can make everything feel normal is to physically touch him.

"Oh, I'm pretty much done. Sorry."

He switches off the tap and rubs the excess water from his body with his hands before opening the glass door and reaching out for his towel. I hand it to him, feeling a bit disappointed.

He steps out and looks at his face in the mirror. "Have you got a big day today?"

"Um…" I have no idea. I feel disoriented. It's going to take me a while to remember my actual life. That dream seemed so real!

Ed pulls on his boxers and golf pants.

"Are you sure you're okay? You look a bit…confused or something."

"I'm all right. I just had a weird dream."

"Ah." He doesn't ask what it was about, and I don't know if I'd want to tell him anyway. It was bad enough when he knew I was reading my diary for a couple of hours. Explaining that I essentially just spent a whole day in 1996 would probably not go down too well.

I sit on the bed and watch while Ed finishes dressing.

"Do you want me to make you some breakfast?"

"Thanks, but I should go. I'll grab a coffee on the way to the golf course."

I hurry over and give him a tight hug, but he pulls away, smoothing down his shirt. I don't think he sees my disappointed reaction.

"Did you want to go out for dinner tonight?" he asks, now combing his hair into position.

My face brightens. "That would be nice."

"I have a client who owns a Japanese restaurant in Hamilton, and he's offered us a free meal. I'll text you the address and you can meet me there later."

"Okay, great." I'm used to Ed's golf days lasting through to the evening, so I wouldn't have expected to see him until at least seven anyway.

He leaves, and I flop down on the couch. I'm feeling unsettled, both by my husband's aversion to touching me, and the events that took place yesterday.

What actually happened between the hours of 10am and 10pm? I glance over at the dining table. My supplement delivery is still lying where I left it.

I hurry over and pick up the Youth Compound. Its label doesn't contain any other information, apart from the small blurb and directions I read yesterday. Shouldn't it at least list the active ingredients? It's Sunday, so I can't call the company and ask. I go into my study and email them instead, requesting further clarification on the product under the guise of wanting to advertise it more thoroughly to my readers.

Whatever was in it was crazy strong if it kept me asleep all day AND all night. They really need to put a warning on it.

Something suddenly occurs to me.

I race into the garage and locate the box from yesterday. I find my diary again and yank it open to yesterday's date.

It's the same entry I read yesterday morning before I passed out. And even though I didn't get a chance to finish reading it, there's enough information in the first half to know it's not the same events I just experienced.

Mum was all mad because I hadn't done enough around the house or something…she has no idea how busy my life is!

Well, obviously that didn't happen this time around, because I offered to do the laundry. And there's no mention of going to The Palace with her. Or meeting Kurt.

So, what does that mean? Maybe I really was just dreaming, and my brain filled in a few extra new details.

I read the last part of the entry that I didn't get to yesterday.

Anyway, I had to work from 4 – 8 tonight and then Kelsey and I went to Rachel's party. That's when things took a turn for the worse…Todd cornered me in Rachel's bedroom and practically forced himself on me. I was totally not ready to sleep with him, and he got really angry when I pushed him away. So, I dropped him. It's kind of a relief in a way. Things were getting way too intense. Now I'm single and free and I can focus on schoolwork for a while. Ha. Yeah right.

Hmm…so last night's outcome was essentially the same. At least it didn't get to the point where I was alone with Todd in Rachel's room.

I carry the diary back inside, skimming through the next few entries, but they don't reveal anything particularly exciting. I glance over at the Youth Compound, wondering what would happen if I took some more. In any event, it's probably not a smart idea to sleep the day away two days in a row. I have a life to attend to here in the present.

I go to the bedroom and put my diary in the bedside drawer, just in case I feel like experimenting later. I slide the Youth Compound in with it and then tidy up the house.

I need to spend some time in reality.

***

The day crawls by, and I can't stop thinking about yesterday. Eventually, I try to distract myself by working on a new recipe—a healthy caramel slice inspired by Grandma Millie's gift. Seeing her again felt so real! I'm not sure if that makes me happy or sad.

I sneak into the bedroom every now and again and read a couple more pages in my diary. I think I might be losing it.

Ed texts just before six with the address for the Japanese restaurant and to say he'll be there by seven. I try and keep my mind focused on the here and now, but it's impossible. Even doing something as simple as straightening my hair reminds me of the crimper I used yesterday. I spritz some Armani Si onto my neck—which was a gift from Ed last birthday— and find myself comparing it to CK One. The Armani doesn't seem to have as many fun memories attached. Hmm...

My outfit tonight is designed to hide my widening hips—a tan dress with an empire-cut waistline that ends just above my knees. I feel myself longing for the perfectly shaped body I had as a sixteen-year-old. I eat well these days and I go to the gym a few times a week, but there's no hiding the fact that age is starting to take its toll.

At six-fifteen, I head down to the city cat and catch it across to Hamilton. When I get to the restaurant, Ed hasn't yet arrived, so I wait alone.

I get out my phone and open Facebook. Without even thinking, my fingers type in Kelsey's name. I find her immediately, thanks to a couple of mutual friends and the fact that she hasn't changed her surname.

Her profile photo is typically her—pretending to kiss the camera. She has her privacy settings set to high, so I can't find out much else. I contemplate sending her a friend request but decide against it for now. She probably still hates me.

"Hey, babe." Ed appears at the table and sits down opposite me.

"Hey."

He leans back in his seat. "Good day?"

"Not too bad. I did a new blog post and tidied up the house."

"That's it?"

I know he doesn't mean to sound uncaring, but Ed has never understood my job. He thinks I spend half an hour actually working, and the rest of the time bumming around. He doesn't know that I have to research stuff, and that social media and marketing are also a big part of what I do.

"I think maybe I was a bit sick," I say to avoid an argument. "My brain wasn't working at full capacity today."

He smiles wryly. "My brain doesn't seem to want to ever work at full capacity." He then rattles on about office politics and how it carried over into his golf day today. A waitress takes our order, and Ed selects all the food. Normally, I wouldn't mind, but today it annoys me. I don't know why.

I study the man I married. He has a strong jaw and a very attractive face with deep blue eyes. His hair is dark blonde, and while it isn't super thick, he knows how to style it to his advantage. If you had shown me a photo of him when I was sixteen, I would have squealed with delight. I don't know about this emotional distance, though. That's definitely not something I'd have been impressed by.

"What?" he says, looking at me.

"What do you mean, *what*?" I say.

"You're staring at me."

"Am I? Sorry." I should try and make an effort to snap out of my mood. "I was just thinking what a hottie I have for a husband."

He laughs. "Oh? Well, I have a pretty hot wife, too. I guess we're both lucky."

I beam. That's more like it. We haven't had a proper conversation in ages. When Ed is busy, I tend to find my own activities to fill the time, rather than asking him to restructure his schedule to allow more opportunities for us to be together. But maybe I should try harder.

"We should plan a trip," I say suddenly.

"Do you think so? Where do you want to go?"

"I don't know. Hawaii?"

He wrinkles his nose. "Hawaii?"

"You don't like Hawaii?"

"I was thinking maybe somewhere a bit more sophisticated. Like Prague."

"Oh. Yeah, Prague sounds nice."

"It just has such great architecture. I would love to go back and take you to my favourite places."

Ed went to Prague when he did a tour of Europe before we met. He talks about it a lot.

"Sure."

"I guess we could do a stopover in Hawaii if you really want to," he concedes.

"No, no. It was just a suggestion." The idea of only being able to spend a day or two in Hawaii sounds worse than not going at all. I would hate to arrive and just start to relax and then have to leave again.

"I'll get my assistant to do some preliminary research for us next week," he says.

"Great."

I should be happier. We're planning a proper holiday. Time away from work and everyday life. It will be awesome.

I just can't help but feel like I don't really get a say. Why does Ed's assistant get to research our holiday? But I can't exactly say I can do it myself, because I just got annoyed that he thinks I have too much free time.

A waitress pours me some wine, and I take a sip.

I'm being silly. Everything is fine.

Completely fine.

SEVEN

I'm woken on Monday morning by Ed making a racket as he finishes showering and changing.

"Is it earlier than usual?" I ask sleepily.

He stands at the foot of the bed, brushing his teeth. "Only a little. I'm going to Melbourne today, remember?"

I sit up. "What?"

"I told you about this weeks ago."

"Are you sure?"

"Of course I'm sure."

"How long are you away for?"

He goes into the bathroom to spit out his toothpaste and talks from there. "Until Friday."

I shake my head as if to rattle the memory loose. Surely I wouldn't have forgotten something like that.

He reappears, doing his tie. "Just stay in bed and relax." He sees my confused expression. "Are you okay?"

"Yeah, I'm fine." I know I'm not acting fine, but I don't know whether to be annoyed at Ed for not telling me about his business trip, or myself for forgetting.

He breezes past, giving me a quick peck on the cheek.

"I'll call you tonight."

I half-heartedly wave and watch him leave.

I don't know if it's because of the events of the last couple of days, but everything feels wrong. Like I don't quite fit.

Maybe I've just noticed that Ed is more standoffish than usual. I'm sure he wasn't always like this. When we first got together, it took him a while to open up, but I know we've shared some genuine intimate moments over the years.

When he gets back at the end of the week, I'm going to make him sit down with me for a proper talk. See what's going on in that brain of his.

I can't go back to sleep, so I lie there and stare at the ceiling. When I hear the front door open and close, I get up and make myself a cup of tea.

I sit at the kitchen counter, thinking about the jar of Youth Compound. If I took it again, would the same thing happen? Was the first time just a one-off delusion? Would I maybe go back to a different point in my personal history? Knowing that the effects don't seem to affect this reality and only last for a day makes it all very tempting.

And if I got the chance to see Grandma Millie again…

Because I worked over the weekend, I don't really need to do another post this morning. Either way, I could always do an extra one tomorrow to make up for it.

I have a quick shower and change into some yoga pants and a comfy T-shirt. I then check my phone to make sure I don't have any messages that need a reply within the next twelve hours. There's one from my mum, thanking me for the gerberas and promising to call me when she has more energy. The rest of my emails aren't urgent and can wait until tomorrow.

I mix up a glass of the foul-tasting concoction and gulp it down as quickly as possible. Knowing that I'll probably start to feel dizzy any moment, I hurry to the bedroom and lie down.

But nothing happens.

How long did it take last time? I guess it was just a strange combination of...

Whoa. Okay. Here we go.

I'm slightly better prepared this time, but still a little scared. What if this stuff has unintended side effects? And what if it's doing permanent damage to my brain?

Too late to worry about that now.

I grab a fistful of bedcovers with each hand as the pressure builds in my head. I have only passed out a couple of times in my life before the other day—one when I had a really bad flu three years ago—and one when I was twenty-one and got drunk on my birthday. Both weren't particularly pleasant, and this isn't either.

I'm unaware of time passing, but I open my eyes after a moment and see that I'm back in 1996. Or at least I assume I am. I'm in my old bedroom this time. The one I was so glad to see again two days ago. I open my diary to confirm the date and see that it's Monday now. The same date as the future. The clock on my bedside cabinet says it's almost 8am.

Someone bangs on the door.

"Anna? Are you up? You're going to be late for school!"

Mum.

"Uh, yeah. I'll be down soon!"

I jump out of bed and put on my uniform. What time does school start? Was it eight thirty or nine?

I quickly stop by the bathroom and brush my teeth. Halfway through, I realise I probably don't need to follow the rules if whatever I do here doesn't change the future. What if I just stayed home? Or cut class? Technically, I should be able to do whatever I want.

I'm just contemplating the possibilities when Mum appears in the doorway.

"Come on, I'll give you a lift this morning. Amy already left half an hour ago."

"Oh, it's okay. I'll walk." A morning at home will give me time to work out how to make the most of the next twelve hours.

"Don't be silly. You don't have time. Grab your stuff. I'm going now."

I want to argue more, but it feels wrong. I don't want 1996 Mum to be mad at me. She was so impressed by my behaviour the other day that I don't want to mess it up now. I mean, there's a chance she might not remember it happened, but still.

"Okay." I figure I can always sneak off the school grounds later.

Mum heads to the garage. I see my school bag near the door and pick it up on the way to join my mother in the car.

My old school is only a couple of minutes' drive away, so I actually end up arriving just as the first bell is ringing. Mum seemed distracted, so I didn't bother striking up a conversation. I was too busy contemplating my next move anyway.

"Are you all right to walk home this afternoon?" she asks as I get out of the car.

"Yep. Thanks. And thanks for the lift!"

I hurry down past the office and hall, and then realise I have no idea where I'm going. I stop and stare at the building where I think the homerooms are located.

There are a few stragglers ahead of me. I recognise one girl who I'm pretty sure was in my homeroom. I follow her to the second floor of the building and to a room at the far right. I know I have a locker, but I can't remember where that might be. Jeez. I should have planned this better.

I leave my bag near the door and hurry over to an empty seat. Everyone else has already arrived. I try and act normally, but it's not easy. I feel so self-conscious and wonder if I've somehow slipped into a more generic dream. All I need now is to look down and discover I'm only in my underwear.

Thankfully, that doesn't happen, but it's still weird. I didn't enjoy school the first time, and I can't imagine I'm going to enjoy it any more now.

Kelsey shoots me a quick smile from the other side of the room. I smile back.

Our teacher, Mr. Simmons, calls the roll.

Ugh. Why am I here?

"Anna?"

"Here."

Mr. Simmons announces a bunch of stuff that means absolutely nothing to me and then excuses us. Kelsey hurries over.

"Are you worried about seeing Todd today?" she asks.

"No. Should I be?"

"Well, you did break his heart the other night. He's probably not going to be in a very good mood."

"That's his problem."

"Ooh. You're tough."

"He did try to force himself on me," I point out. Something occurs to me. "Hey, on Saturday morning, do you remember what we talked about?"

She wrinkles her nose. "What do you mean?"

"Was I acting weird on Saturday morning?"

"You're always acting weird. You're going to have to be more specific."

"Was I asking what date it was and saying I looked really young?"

She raises an eyebrow. "Not that I can recall, but I *was* half asleep most of the morning. You probably could have said anything, and I wouldn't have noticed. Why?"

"No reason."

Okay. So, it looks like the timeline from the other day isn't the same as the one I'm in now. Before Rachel's party, Kelsey made a point of mentioning how bizarrely I'd been acting that morning, so it's unlikely she would have forgotten about it so soon afterwards. I might have to test my theory again at some point, though, just to be sure.

I follow Kelsey outside and grab my bag. She looks down at it. "Running late today, huh?"

"Uh, yeah."

"Cramming in some last-minute study for the chemistry test? I am totally going to fail. I was going to study last night, but then Andy got home, and he invited his friends over and we all ended up getting high…"

Chemistry test? There's no way I'm sitting a chemistry test.

"I think I'm going to go home," I say.

Her eyes widen. "Why?"

"Because I don't want to do the test."

She laughs. "I don't either, but it's not like we have a choice."

I do, but I can't tell *her* that.

"You should go. I'll see you there," I say.

She narrows her eyes. "Really?"

"Yeah. I'm just going to stop by the bathroom first."

I know I don't sound very convincing, but there's not enough time for her to argue with me further.

She shrugs. "Suit yourself."

I head off in the opposite direction and down to the school's back exit. I figure I'm less likely to see anyone that way.

I'm just at the gate when I hear someone call out.

"Miss Parnell!"

I spin around, despite Parnell not being my surname anymore. Damn. It's the principal. What was his name? Mr. Quinn?

"Uh, yeah?"

"Where do you think you're going? Class is that way." He points to the building behind him.

"I forgot my textbooks," I say lamely.

"Well, I'm sure you can get by without them this morning. Someone will share with you if need be."

"I also forgot my lunch," I try.

His mouth pinches into a disapproving O. "Miss Parnell, I thought you were one of our good students. Do I need to reconsider my assessment?"

God. This is definitely not how I envisioned spending my morning. And while it's tempting to tell my old school principal to get lost, I don't want to screw up the rest of the day. There's also an overwhelming force compelling me to do the right thing. I'm not sure if that's just who I am, or if the compound has something to do with it.

I cave. "I'm sorry, Mr. Quinn. I'm just going through a tough time at the moment."

His face softens. "How about you go off to class then, and at recess you can visit the counsellor? She might be able to give you some guidance."

"Okay," I agree.

He waves his hand to usher me back in the direction I just came. "Better hurry."

I take my time walking away from the gate and freedom. I'm starting to think coming back to 1996 again was a mistake. I can't imagine my day here is going to be more fun than a Monday spent alone in Brisbane without anyone telling me what to do.

Mr. Quinn walks behind me. I have no idea where the chemistry lab is, so I open my bag and rummage around inside, searching for clues. It looks like I did, in fact, forget my books AND lunch, so I wasn't lying. But my school diary is in my bag and it thankfully has my timetable on it.

Monday at 9am: Chemistry in S2. Where's S2?

"What's your first class?" Mr. Quinn asks.

"Chemistry in S2."

He nods. "I'll see that you get there without any detours."

Great. Mr. Quinn can lead the way.

We reach the room, and he opens the door.

"I have a straggler for you, Joe," he says, moving aside to let me in.

The entire class looks up.

Joe, or Mr. Green as I remember him, frowns. "You've interrupted the students and missed the first ten minutes of your exam. Sit."

I meekly sit down in the last available seat. Kelsey gives me a bemused look. Everyone else turns back to their test papers.

As Mr. Quinn leaves, his expression seems to be one of annoyance and pity.

Mr. Green slaps down an exam booklet in front of me. "You will not get a time extension," he says quietly.

I nod. It's not going to make a difference anyway. I have no idea how to answer any of these questions. Luckily, it doesn't actually matter.

I spend the next half hour staring at the unanswered exam. I was never any good at chemistry the first time around, and that was even with study. This time, it all looks like a foreign language.

Instead, I think about what other things might not have mattered in my original timeline. How many events or situations affected where I ended up? Is everything so finely balanced that even the slightest variation could change the future? I'm kind of glad I'll never know. At least not by using the Youth Compound.

When the bell goes, I hand in my blank paper. Mr. Green looks at it and then up at me.

"Detention. Recess. Here."

I nod. But I don't mean it.

Screw this. I grab my bag and head out to the back gate again.

This time, I'm not stopping for anybody.

EIGHT

Ten minutes later, I arrive home and let myself in. The house is blissfully empty. I help myself to a glass of milk and some cookies and sit down at the breakfast bar.

Ah. This is more like it. School is awful. I can't believe I survived thirteen years of it without any permanent emotional scarring. As far as I'm aware.

Outside, the sun blazes down. It's supposed to be winter, but the walk back was surprisingly warm.

Hmm…maybe I should go down to the beach. And why not? The one thing I could not easily do if I was in Brisbane is spend the day at the beach—at least without a lot of driving.

I run upstairs and change into my bikini. That's another thing I couldn't do in the future—wear such a tiny swimsuit with confidence. I didn't appreciate my body nearly enough when I was this age. I took it for granted that I would be skinny forever without trying.

After grabbing a towel and checking to see if Mum or Dad left a car behind (they didn't), I call a cab.

Down on Shell Beach, I find a spot on the sand and lie in the sun, feeling much better about my decision to use the compound again. This is what I should have been doing all along. The ocean is a shimmery blue-green and there isn't a cloud in the sky. While the water is chilly, the air temperature is perfect.

I glance back at the scenery behind me. I haven't spent a lot of time here in recent years because the town has changed, and not in a good way in my opinion. Right now, all I can see are a few low-set, family-friendly resorts, and a handful of houses around the point. In the future, the family-friendly resorts are made over to cater to the Sydney and Melbourne hipster crowds, and the rich visitors who decided to stay permanently have built mansions around the point. I often wondered if I had rose-tinted glasses on when it came to preferring nineties Shell Beach to the current one, but it turns out I was right to think that way.

I lie back on my towel and close my eyes. This is the life.

"Heads up!" I hear the warning too late, and suddenly there's a flurry of sand and a large body falling on top of me.

"Oh my God, I am so sorry!"

I have sand in my eyes, so I don't respond immediately. I use the corner of my towel to wipe my face and try to blink the irritation out. I think my side might be bruised.

"What the hell?" I complain.

"Are you okay?" the voice asks. It sounds vaguely familiar. "I was trying to make sure my Frisbee didn't clonk you on the head, but I think it would have caused less damage than me."

I manage to open my eyes properly and look at the person now watching me with concern. I jump with shock.

"Kurt!"

His face is confused. "Do I know you?"

"It's me, Anna. From the record store the other day!"

He nods slowly. "Well, I do work at a record store, but I guess I serve so many people, I might accidentally forget some of them. I'm sorry."

I'm just about to mention the whole listening-to-vinyl-together thing when I catch myself. I think along with Kelsey's lack of memory, Kurt's reaction definitely confirms I'm in a different timeline to the other day.

"Oh. Never mind. I just...um...assumed you would have recognised me."

He squints at my face and smiles. "Well, I'm an idiot for not remembering someone as pretty as you."

I blush and then point to a couple of guys further up the sand, obviously waiting for Kurt to re-join the game. "I think your friends are getting impatient."

He reluctantly collects his Frisbee and stands up. "I guess I should go. But I promise to remember you next time you visit the music store. You said your name was Anna?"

"That's right."

"Okay, Anna. I am mentally taking a photo of your face, so I'll never forget it again." He stares at me for a second, a half-smile playing on his lips, and then walks away.

My stomach fizzes. I blame sixteen-year-old hormones seeping through. But also, who wouldn't be flattered by a cute guy flirting with them?

I watch Kurt and his friends from a distance but redirect my thoughts back to this timeline situation. It appears that I'm one step closer to understanding how it all works. But what's the point of taking the compound if I can't change the future? And if I can't even set up an event in this new 1996 and see it through the next time, why bother at all?

Also, if it's not actually a dream, but some portal I'm accessing via the compound, does this version of reality continue on its own trajectory after I leave? Or does it only exist while I'm here and disappear when I wake up?

I look at my watch. It's not even lunchtime, so there's still plenty of time to contemplate these things and work out the best way to spend the rest of the day.

But for now, I think I just want to enjoy the sun.

I lie back down and close my eyes again.

Ah.

This is definitely better than a day alone in Brisbane.

***

I enjoy a leisurely couple of hours relaxing on the beach and then walk up Main Street, looking in all the shops that are long gone in the future. Like the cute little convenience store that sells bags of mixed sweets for fifty cents and rents out old eighties comedies like *Big* and *Twins*. Or the T-shirt shop where my friend Rachel works on the weekends. It pretty much only sells T-shirts embroidered with the words *Shell Beach*. And then there's the cheesy resort clothing boutiques that in the future are designer stores like Boss and Tigerlily.

I finally stop in at Beans, the coffee shop I used to practically live at as a teenager. I can't remember the last time I was here.

I go up to the counter and order a soy chai latte. The waiter, who I don't think I remember, looks at me strangely. "A what?"

Oops. Clearly, chai lattes didn't make it to Shell Beach until after 1996.

"Um, just a hot chocolate is fine," I say hastily. Normally, I drink double shot espressos, but I don't feel like I need the caffeine boost in this body.

"That'll be three dollars, please," he says.

I hand over my coins. Very reasonable for a drink on a busy tourist street.

"Anna!"

I turn to the voice and see Jackson, a waiter I once had a crush on. I eventually found out he was gay, so I had to re-channel that energy into a more platonic admiration.

"Hi, Jackson." Man, why didn't I stay in touch with this guy? He was so awesome. I can imagine we would have had a lot of fun hanging out together.

"Why aren't you at school?" he asks mock sternly.

"Uh, long story," I say.

"I'm about to have a break. You want to keep me company?"

"Sure."

I collect my hot chocolate and go sit at a small table near the back, away from the street. I take a sip of my drink and wait for Jackson to join me.

My phone rings. I don't recognise the number, but it could be Kelsey calling from the public phone booth at school, so I answer.

"Hello?"

"Where the hell are you?"

Yep. Definitely Kelsey. "Down on Main Street. Why? Where are you?"

"Um, I'm at school. Why aren't you?"

"I didn't feel like being there today."

"What's going on with you, Anna? You never cut class. Mr. Green was looking for you because you didn't show up for detention. Your parents will flip out if he calls them."

"It'll all be fine. You want to come and join me?"

"Ha, no thanks. You should come back and join *me*."

"Nah. Whatever trouble I'm in, it probably won't get any worse if I don't go back."

"This is really not like you."

"Well, maybe I don't want to spend such a beautiful day inside doing work that isn't going to have any effect on my life in two years' time."

Jackson sits down opposite me, holding a drink for himself.

"The bell has just gone, so I have to go, but I'll call you again after school. Then you can tell me what's really going on," Kelsey says.

"I'm not hiding anything, but okay. Later!"

Jackson raises an eyebrow. "Everything all right?"

"Yeah. Just Kelsey wondering why I'm not at school."

"And there's no other reason you're cutting that you're not saying?"

"Apart from it being boring as hell?"

He laughs. "I hated school, too, but I was never any good at it. I'm betting you are."

"I did…I mean, I do okay."

"What do you want to do after you graduate?"

"I'm going to study to be a pastry chef in Paris. I don't really need to get amazing grades for that. I just need to be able to pay for the course. And get there."

"It sounds like you have it all figured out."

I'm not going to brag, but I actually did. My final academic results were good, but they didn't really need to be. I started saving part of my pay from the video store in year twelve, and then I stayed on to work there full-time for most of the year after. That gave me enough money to get to France in October, 1998.

I'm interested to get Jackson's take on the workings of the universe. Maybe he knows something I don't.

"People think everything is so life and death. What if it isn't?"

He laughs. "This is what I like about you, Anna. You are not a typical sixteen-year-old."

I smile. I like to think I was a bit more mature than my friends the first time around, but I probably wasn't.

"I'm serious. Do you think life is full of decisions you have to get right?"

"Yes and no."

"Do you have any regrets?"

"Not really. I'm only twenty-one, so nothing is really set in stone yet."

"True."

I think about my future life. I'm starting to get to a point where some options are almost closed to me. Like being a supermodel. Ha. Or a pop star. Or a famous athlete. Obviously, nothing is impossible, but the odds are now stacked against me. Still, I'm mostly happy with where I ended up. Ed and I decided we didn't want kids, so I don't have to worry about that option closing off.

He thinks for a second. "I do sometimes wonder how each decision affects the next moment. I don't mean that if you're horrible to someone, something bad will happen to you, because I think that's bullshit—but say if I decided to move to Brisbane instead of staying here in Shell Beach, would my life be permanently on another path? Or would I eventually come back to the same place I was going to end up anyway?"

"That's exactly what I've been wondering lately. And I have no idea. I think maybe there are some big choices that can have an impact on what ultimately happens, but maybe the smaller ones don't matter so much. Then again, who knows? Maybe the universe has a clever way of getting you back on track no matter what you decide."

"I don't know if I like the idea of a preconceived destiny, because that means there's not really any free will."

"But would you know? There's no way of testing whether something else could have happened."

He takes a gulp of his drink and winces. It looks like a long black, so I'm guessing it's hot and strong. "This is a bit deep for a Monday."

"It is. But I'm glad you want to talk about this stuff. I don't really know anyone else who wonders why things are the way they are."

After I say it, I realise it's true—especially in the future. Ed hates to have deep conversations, but it's usually because he's too tired from work and just wants to switch off. And I don't really have that many close friends. I have lots of acquaintances, and certainly lots of fans from my work, but now that I think about it, I don't have anyone I feel this comfortable with talking about the meaning of life.

"Where do you think you'll be in twenty years?" I ask suddenly.

He laughs. "That came out of the blue. Um, I guess I'll have already turned forty. Hopefully, I have a high-paying job, an awesome house, and someone who loves me."

I smile. "That sounds like a great plan. Do you think you'll still be in Shell Beach?"

"Who knows? But probably not. There aren't a lot of…" he trails off. I can tell he's wondering whether I know he's gay or not.

"Cute boys who also like boys?" I finish for him.

He chuckles, relieved. "That's right. I might head to Brisbane one of these days. Or maybe Melbourne."

"Do whatever makes you happiest."

He finishes his drink and stands up. He comes over to my side of the table and pulls me up, giving me a huge hug. "You're awesome, Anna. I'm glad you cut class today. I just hope you don't get into too much trouble."

"I'll be fine. I'm glad we got to hang out."

"When do you turn eighteen? I'm going to take you out dancing."

"Not for another year and a bit."

"Well, keep me posted. You have a date whenever you need one."

Even though I know I'll never be able to take Jackson up on his offer, I still feel all warm and fuzzy.

"Will do."

We say our farewells, and I head off home.

This visit to 1996 was a pretty good idea after all.

NINE

Uh-oh.

I'd planned on going home to change before heading out to visit Grandma Millie, but when I walk through the door, my mum is standing in the kitchen, talking to someone on the phone. She does not look pleased.

"Thank you, she's just arrived. I'll talk to her now." She hangs up and crosses her arms. "Anna! Where have you been? I just got a call from the school. Apparently, you were late to class, got found trying to sneak out by the principal, handed in a blank test, and then disappeared! What on earth has gotten into you?"

"If I told you, you wouldn't believe me."

She narrows her eyes. "Try me."

For a moment I wonder what would happen if I actually revealed the truth. That I'm a grown woman trapped in a sixteen-year-old's body. She'd probably have me committed.

What would be a normal response for a teenage girl who was seemingly rebelling against the system?

"I think I might be pregnant," I blurt out. Shit. Why did I say that?

Mum's eyes widen. "You're what?"

"I'm probably not," I assure her. Jeez. I hadn't even lost my virginity in 1996. What am I doing to the me in this reality? And my poor mother!

There goes all the goodwill I built up the other day.

"Don't tell me Todd is the father," she says, looking sick at the thought.

"Uh, no. You don't know him."

What am I doing?

"I don't know if that's worse. Honey! How could this happen? Weren't you safe?"

"Yes, but accidents happen."

She marches over to the phone. "I'm making an appointment at the doctor so we can figure out what to do."

"No, no. Not today. Can we leave it at least until tomorrow? Or the next day?"

She shakes her head. "No, the sooner the better. We'll need to book you in for a scan and find out how far along you are. When did you last get your period?"

Crap. Why the hell did I say I was pregnant?

"Um…six weeks ago?" I really have no idea.

She loosens her grip on the phone. "Then it's still very early days. It might just be that your cycle is messed up. Have you taken a pregnancy test?"

"No."

"Maybe we should do that first." She picks up her handbag. "Come on, we'll go buy one now."

"I'm not feeling very well. Do you mind if I lie down, and we can go a bit later?"

"I'll go. You stay and rest up. I'll be back in half an hour."

"Okay. Thanks, Mum."

As she leaves, she gives me a look full of fear and disappointment.

I feel awful, but I can't do much about it right now. However, I can try and limit the damage I've done. I scrawl an apology on a piece of paper, saying that I got my period just after she left and that I went for a walk to clear my head.

I go upstairs to change into something a bit warmer and then lock up the house, walking in the opposite direction to the one I know Mum drove. I've kind of screwed up today, so maybe I should push it further and see what happens.

My first test will be with Kelsey. I glance at my watch. I'll go to her house and wait out the front until she finishes school.

Operation Fuck Up Anna's Life is about to commence.

***

I walk all the way to Kelsey's because I know she won't be home until after three and I need to fill in some time. I thought about still going to visit Grandma Millie, but the next bus to Maroochydore wasn't for ages, and by the time I got there, visiting hours at the retirement home would almost be over. I sigh. I think I feel worse about not seeing her than lying to my mother about being pregnant.

Kelsey arrives at her house the same time as me. "Hey, you. Come in. I expect you to tell me everything."

I nod. I've decided I'm going to be totally honest with her and see what happens.

Andy is inside, sitting at the dining table and eating a sandwich. He gives me that gross look again. I decide to bluff and see what happens.

"Andy, I'd get rid of that stash in your room if I were you. You don't know when the cops might drop by unannounced."

He scowls. "What the fuck are you talking about?"

"I don't think they'd take kindly to some of the...pharmaceuticals...you own."

His face goes white. "You stay the fuck out of my room. And if the cops do come around, I'll be looking for you soon after."

Kelsey stares at me in shock. "What's going on?"

"Nothing," I say, and head upstairs. It seems I was right. He was already into that stuff, even in 1996.

Andy jumps up and follows us.

"Relax, I'm not going to touch your Rohypnol," I call over my shoulder.

Kelsey gasps. "Rohypnol?"

Andy shoves past us and storms into his room, slamming the door behind him.

"What the hell is going on, Anna?"

I enter her room and point to her bed. "You should probably sit down. You're going to think I'm nuts in a couple of seconds."

"I already do, babe. I already do." She sits down anyway.

"I don't even know where to start," I say. "Okay, so I'm not actually sixteen. I'm in my late thirties."

Her face goes blank for a second, and then she looks annoyed. "Is this like *Candid Camera* or something?"

"No. I promise. I'm from the future."

"Riiight…so what's the purpose of telling me this?" I can see she still doesn't believe me, but she's playing along. For now.

"I guess I was tired of not being able to tell anyone. Do you have any questions?"

"A ton. But mostly I'm wondering whether I should phone emergency services and get them to take you away to be assessed."

"I'm not dangerous."

"But you've obviously got some mental health issues. And what was that whole thing with Andy just now?"

"In the future, he gets arrested for drug possession and spiking girls' drinks."

Kelsey's face collapses. "Why would you say that?"

"Because it's true. And judging by his reaction a moment ago, you could probably find proof in his bedroom if you went in there right now."

She looks sick. "Okay. Well, let's pretend for a second that what you're saying is true. When does this happen? Him getting caught, I mean?"

"I don't know the exact dates. You and I…"

"What?"

"We don't really talk in the future."

Now she looks eerily calm. "How come?"

"You thought I slept with one of your boyfriends."

Her eyes almost bug out. "And did you?"

"No. But I couldn't change your mind. You believed the guy over me."

"When does this supposedly happen?"

"In 2000."

"You mean we never speak again after that?"

"That's right."

"Prove to me that you're not making everything up."

"I can't. Unless Andy lets you in his room."

"Yeah, but how do I know you didn't just go snooping around in there the other morning?"

"Either way, it's drugs, Kelsey! And who knows what else? Your brother has serious issues."

I can tell her head is spinning. "All right. If that's the case, what should I do with this information?"

"I don't know. He's going to get arrested eventually. You could maybe call the police and get them to take him away now. It might stop him from hurting any other women."

At least in this version of reality.

She gives me a troubled look. "I don't know if I can do that. At least

75

not until I confront him about it."

"You do what you have to."

"How does this time travel thing work, anyway?"

"I haven't completely figured it out, but basically I took a supplement in my time that made me black out and wake up here. I guess it's some sort of hallucinogenic dream where I have full control over my decisions. And so far, it seems like nothing I do here affects the future. I can only come back for twelve hours at a time, and then the next time I return, nothing that happened the last time seems to have even occurred."

"What happens after twelve hours? Do you just disappear?"

"I don't know. Either this is a version of reality I've somehow slipped into temporarily and the sixteen-year-old me will take over when I leave, or it will cease to exist altogether because it's just a product of my imagination."

Kelsey looks like her brain might explode. "What?"

"I could tell you what the future's like? I mean, not for you personally, but what's happening in the world."

Now she looks bemused.

"Okay. Tell me what the world is like in your time."

I try to think of all the events of the last twenty-odd years.

"Uh, do you know Donald Trump?"

She wrinkles her nose. "That rich guy in America?"

"Yeah. I guess you would know him as a famous tycoon from the eighties?"

"What about him?"

"He's the US president. Hillary Clinton was his opponent, and everyone thought she was going to win."

"You mean the wife of the current US president?"

"Yep."

She shakes her head. "Weird."

"And we have a female prime minister here for a short while. Aussie politics get pretty messed up and they seem to change prime ministers every few months."

"I hate politics." She looks like she's finally warming to the idea of finding out more, even if she thinks I might be making it all up. "Tell me about my life until we stopped being friends."

"Are you sure you want to know?"

"Yes! Do I meet a cute guy? What do I do?"

I think back. "Um, you hadn't really settled down. You had a couple of relationships, but they didn't work out."

"What were their names? I can look out for them when they show up."

"One of them was called Mark. You met him at the Ocean Club when we were out one night. He was cute, but he had a bit of a drug problem. You broke up with him when you caught him shooting up."

She looks horrified. "So, I could have contracted hepatitis or HIV?"

"I'm assuming you were safe when you slept together, but either way, you didn't seem to have any health issues when we stopped talking."

"What about the other guy I went out with?"

"His name was Robert. He was really charismatic, but he cheated on you after six months."

She shakes her head. "Jesus. Can you tell me something nice that happened?"

"What do you want to do once you graduate? Career-wise, I mean."

"Be a fashion designer, of course."

"Oh, that's right. Well, you change your mind at the end of next year and decide to be a teacher instead. Which is lucky, because the fashion industry kind of falls apart in the future and it's really hard to make any money from it."

She throws up her hands. "Just kill me now. I want to be a teacher?"

"Yeah. And you do really well at university. You already had a full-time placement near Indooroopilly lined up when we stopped talking, so I'm pretty sure you would have kicked butt."

"But you don't actually know."

"No."

"At least I'm down in Brisbane and not stuck here in Shell Beach. I wish you could go back to the future and come back to tell me what I'm doing now."

"Well, I could, only you won't remember this conversation."

She frowns. "That sucks."

"It does," I agree. "If I can't change the version of the future I'm from, I don't really see the point of coming back. Especially when I don't have any continuity when I do return."

"It *does* seem pretty useless. I wonder if there's a way to contact future me. Can you track me down? Or have I disappeared off the face of the earth?"

"Oh, you can pretty much find anyone these days. There's this website called Facebook, and nearly everyone has a profile page where they post photos and comments and talk to everyone else."

"A website? So, the internet becomes popular? And even people like Andy have a page?"

"Yep."

"Andy doesn't even know how to switch on a computer."

"Andy will probably get quite good at using technology in the future, because it's where he'll be able to hook up with women anonymously. There are dozens of sites where people go just to find someone to have sex with. There are even ones for married people to have affairs."

She shakes her head. "The future sounds horrible. Please tell me they at least have flying cars and hoverboards?"

"No. They have a type of self-balancing scooter called a hoverboard, but it's nothing like the ones in *Back to the Future*. And we're still a ways off from having flying cars. But they do have electric ones that you don't need petrol for. And they also have driverless cars, only they're still in the experimental phase."

"That is so cool! Driverless cars! Tell me more!"

Kelsey now doesn't seem to care whether I'm telling the truth or not. I indulge her and we spend an hour talking about pop culture...about the rise of stars like Britney Spears, Justin Timberlake, and then Kanye West...and how there's a possibility that even *he* could run for US president one day. I assure her that we don't have another world war, at least not before my time, but there are many conflicts in the Middle East.

And then I remember 9/11.

"In 2001, terrorists hijack some planes and crash them into the Twin Towers in New York. The buildings completely collapse, and thousands of people die."

She looks horrified. "Seriously?"

"Yeah. It felt like the whole world changed after that. There was a lot of fear, and all these new laws were introduced. Now when you book a flight, you have to take your shoes off at the airport so security can check you're not carrying weapons...and you can't take drinks onto the plane...they also have full-body scanners..."

"It sounds like *Total Recall*."

"It is in a way. Oh, and not to sound flippant, but you just reminded me. They remake that movie and it's terrible. Don't bother watching it. But they are planning on colonising Mars for real. Except anyone who goes won't be able to return to Earth because the trip is so long."

"All right, all right. I think I need a break from this craziness. There's too much to know about the future. And that's assuming what you're saying is actually true."

"I promise it's true—at least in my version of the future. Who knows? Maybe your version will be different. If you continue to exist after I leave, maybe you can use this information for good. I'd like to think that the future isn't necessarily predetermined."

She thinks for a second. "You say you can't change the future from here, but what if you can use the information you gained here to change it back there?"

"In what way?"

"I mean, for example, talk to future me. Convince me that you didn't sleep with that guy I dated. Tell her that you met me back here and that she needs to forgive you."

"You probably won't believe me. Unless there's some secret you never told me I can use as proof."

"Hmm...I pretty much tell you everything already." She rubs her temples.

After a moment, she claps her hands. "I know! My secret crush is Mr. Green."

I laugh. "What?"

"Yep. I've never told anyone that. Even you until now. Tell future Kelsey, and she will believe anything you say."

"You're in love with our chemistry teacher? How? And why?" Even as an adult, I can't see the appeal. He's so...beige.

"I don't know, I just like him. And don't you dare tell anyone at school. I'm trusting you here."

"You're insane."

"Hey, I think today, of all days, you can't be saying things like that."

"Sorry. That's true."

"Do you think you might come back to 1996 again?"

"I'm not sure yet."

"Well, if you do, you can always tell me about Mr. Green. It'll be a way to fast forward through all the convincing you had to do just now. Hey, it's like *Groundhog Day* and you're Bill Murray."

"I guess it is. Kind of."

"Except you're not trying to impress Andie MacDowell."

I blush. I can't help it. My brain automatically goes to Kurt.

Kelsey notices. "What?"

"Nothing. I mean, if I explain, you'll get the wrong idea."

"No! Tell me!"

I sigh. "I met this guy the other day when I was at The Palace, and I saw him down at the beach again today, but he didn't remember me. So, he was sort of like Andie MacDowell's character in *Groundhog Day*."

She grins. "Ooh…interesting. Is he cute?"

"He's not bad looking," I admit.

"So, what's the problem? Do you have a boyfriend in the future or something?"

"Yes. I have a lovely husband called Ed."

She looks like she can't get her head around it. "You're actually married?"

"Well, most people are married by their thirties."

"I know, but I can't believe you're that old! You don't talk any differently. Apart from this future stuff, obviously. But you still sound like you. Do you have kids?"

"No. Ed and I decided we didn't want them."

"Oh. I wonder if I had them?"

"I'm not sure. Sorry."

"That's okay. Well, I suppose we should make the most of the remaining hours you have here. What do you want to do?"

"I don't know. I can't go home. Mum heard about me cutting class, and I told her I was pregnant."

Kelsey roars with laughter. "You what?"

"It was the first thing that popped into my head. I know it was a dumb thing to say, but it's obviously not true. I hope I haven't ruined anything for this version of Anna."

"But then maybe we'll all forget what happened by tomorrow and we'll still think your original version of 1996 exists."

"Actually, I hadn't thought of that. I really wish there was a manual for this situation."

"Either way, I say we go out and have some fun. I'll get you reacquainted with 1996 and you can tell me more about this crazy future you're from. You say the fashion industry has kind of collapsed. Is that because everyone wears a generic bronze-coloured uniform or something?"

I laugh. "No. I'm not sure why high fashion is in trouble, but maybe it's because you can buy everything on the internet now, and if you still want to go to the shops, there are lots of massive boutiques that sell really cheap clothes. Everything is instantly available."

She shakes her head. "So, what do you wear in the future?"

"It's actually not *that* much different from now. In fact, all the teenagers are wearing nineties-inspired stuff at the moment. But all pop culture kind of fractured into lots of little sub-groups, so anything goes, really."

"Oh."

"For example, we have people called hipsters. It started out where it wasn't cool to be called a hipster, but now it's pretty much normal. The guys have huge beards and tie their hair up in buns. Oh, and then there's the activewear mums who buy expensive leggings and workout gear even if they're not going to the gym."

She rolls her eyes. "It sounds awesome. Not."

We grab our bags and head outside.

"I'm not going to disagree with you there."

TEN

Shell Beach is a small town, and Main Street is pretty much the only destination for teenagers, so when Kelsey suggests we go back there for the evening, I agree. But I do ask that we eat somewhere other than Beans. Kelsey is fine with that and chooses a little restaurant overlooking the beach.

"I want to know more about the future. Tell me everything you can think of!"

"Do you want to know about all the celebrities who die?"

"That's a bit depressing, but okay."

"Um…Princess Diana dies next year in a car crash in Paris with her boyfriend, because the paparazzi were chasing them…"

"Oh my God! That's horrible!"

"I know. The whole world can tell you where they were when they heard the news. Also, Steve Irwin is killed by a stingray."

"Who's Steve Irwin?"

"Oh. Yeah, you might not have heard of him yet. He's this crazy Aussie guy they call the Crocodile Hunter. He gets really popular in the States before becoming famous back here."

She wrinkles her nose. "I might have heard of him?"

"Believe me, he'll be all over the TV soon if he isn't already. Oh…and Michael Jackson and Prince die."

Her face is shocked. "When?"

"I'm not sure of the exact dates, but Michael Jackson was a few years ago now. Some lethal combination of prescribed drugs, I think. And Prince only died in 2016. Drugs, too, I'm pretty sure."

"What about Madonna? Please tell me she's okay."

"Yeah, she's still doing her thing. She controversial as always, but now it's because she's older and still prancing around half naked on stage. I think it's pretty cool, though."

Kelsey laughs. "That's awesome."

"2016 was an interesting year. Along with Prince, David Bowie died, and so did Alan Rickman. You might know him from *Die Hard* and *Robin Hood*, but soon he's going to be Professor Snape in a series of movies called *Harry Potter*. They're based on these books that are basically the most popular thing since *Lord of the Rings*."

"I have to be honest. I'm still not totally convinced you're from the future, but either way, this is all very entertaining!"

"As long as you give me the benefit of the doubt, that's all I can ask for. I'm glad we're spending the afternoon together."

She reaches over and hugs me. "Me, too. But can I call you Psycho Woman?"

"If you like. I won't be offended."

We head into the café and sit right on the edge of the boardwalk overlooking the ocean.

"You know in the future, this place charges almost fifty dollars for a steak? And twenty dollars for a dessert?"

Kelsey shakes her head. "I don't know if I like the sound of the future."

"There are lots of good things, too."

"Like what?"

I actually have to stop and think. "Well, the internet makes life really convenient. I already told you that you can buy clothes on there, and track down pretty much anyone you want, but you can also read the news, listen to any song, and watch any movie."

"What—for free?"

"Not quite. Some stuff you still need to pay for. But there's this thing called YouTube that has millions of video clips people have uploaded, and you can watch most of them for free. But there's a huge problem with piracy, so the movie and music industries are in trouble, because they aren't making as much money anymore."

"That sounds like a bad thing. I thought you were going to tell me good things!"

"Right. Um…I guess it's hard to explain. I mean, there are a ton of fun things I end up doing on a personal level. Like travelling overseas…and my job is really cool. I get paid to post blogs about food."

"What's a blog?"

"Oh, like an online diary. I make healthy desserts and take photos of them, and then I post them on the internet."

"And you actually get paid to do that?"

"Yeah. A lot of people do it and don't get paid, but I'm lucky."

"Cool."

"Anyway, let's have a break from talking about the future. Tell me about now. What's the latest?"

She thinks for a minute. "I'm in love with Aaron."

I laugh. "I already knew that. When I came back the other day we went to Rachel's party and you were hoping he was there."

"Oh. Well, then I guess you know he wasn't."

"Actually, I didn't. I ended up being cornered by Todd and then passed out."

"So, you still had the same thing happen as the first time?"

"Almost. I didn't let him get me alone in a bedroom, though."

"That's hilarious."

"I beg to differ."

"Sorry, I didn't mean that what Todd did was hilarious, just that you seem to be reliving the same things."

Not everything.

"It's fine. I know what you meant."

"Okay, I guess I don't know what to tell you. You already experienced it the first time, so I can't tell you much new."

"How about we just eat and enjoy now? Whatever this time is?"

"Sounds good to me."

We each order a hamburger with fries, and a Coke. Kelsey looks thoughtful.

"What?" I ask.

"I just really hope we can be friends again in the future."

"Me, too. I'll make it happen."

She looks at her watch. "What time are you supposed to leave or whatever?"

"8pm, probably."

"Kind of like the Cinderella pumpkin thing, but a few hours earlier."

"Yep. This is all just a dream."

"I'm pretty sure it's not a dream."

"Says the figment of my imagination."

"Don't say that! It's happening, so it's real."

"Okay. We'll act like that's the case, regardless of whether it is or not."

"Thank you. Hey, before you were talking about US pop culture and politics a lot. How come?"

"I guess because the world is so connected with the internet, we're exposed to all their news. I thought it was like that now."

"I'm not sure it's as bad as what it is in your time."

"Just you wait until you learn about the Kardashians."

"The what?"

"And reality TV. Sorry, I know I wasn't going to talk more about the future, but I can't stop comparing then to now. In the future, more than half the TV shows are reality TV. They have cooking competitions, house renovation competitions, dating competitions…"

"Like *Perfect Match*?"

"No, this is *Perfect Match* on steroids. They get one guy and twenty-five women, and they have to fight to be chosen by the guy. Each week, some of them get eliminated until there's only one left."

"Sounds awful."

"It's strangely addictive, but yes, it's pretty bad."

Kelsey is staring at something behind me.

"Hey," she nudges me with her elbow. "Check out the hot guy over there."

I turn my head to see who she means.

My heart stops. Of course.

"You mean the guy with the long dark hair?" I ask, still looking at him and trying not to move my lips.

"Yep."

"That's Kurt."

"Who?"

"The guy I was telling you about before."

She shrieks in glee, which of course causes him to look in our direction. I quickly turn away, but I know he's seen me. Damn.

"He's coming over," she whispers.

"Thanks a lot," I mutter.

I try to slide down in my chair, but it's not like we're in a booth or anything. I'm completely exposed.

"Hey. Fancy seeing you here."

I look up with an embarrassed smile.

"We were just stalking you," Kelsey jokes.

He looks at me questioningly. "Is that right?"

"No. I promise we weren't," I hurriedly assure him.

"Really?" His eyes are twinkling. Oh God.

Kelsey cuts in. "I was kidding. This place was my suggestion. We actually had no idea you'd be here."

He keeps looking at me. "Oh. That's a shame."

Kelsey decides to take matters into her own hands. "Well, of course if we *had* known you were going to be here, we definitely would have chosen it on purpose."

I give her an exasperated look.

He laughs. "Well, I'd invite you both to join me and the guys, but we were just paying our bill. We're not in a hurry to go home, though, so do you want to meet us out on the boardwalk when you're done?"

"Sure!" Kelsey answers before I can protest.

"Great. Take your time. See you in a bit."

He walks off, and Kelsey turns to me, her eyes shining. "Wow. He's a total babe. Well done."

"What are you doing?" I hiss. "I'm married, remember? Besides, he's much too young for me. My next landmark birthday is forty."

"So, you can have a toy-boy. And didn't you just say this is all a dream? If he doesn't technically exist, you can't feel guilty. I mean, have you ever felt bad for making out with Leonardo DiCaprio in any of your other dreams?"

Despite my annoyance, I laugh. I didn't realise my celebrity obsession had been so enduring. "For the record, Leonardo is still cool in my time.

And no, I don't feel guilty about celebrity dreams. I understand your point, but this feels different. I have control over what happens, so I'm not going to choose to cheat on my husband."

"Whatever. But if it were me, I would be taking full advantage of the situation. We can't be rude anyway, so we'll have to at least say hello after we finish eating."

"Fine. But we're only staying for a couple of minutes."

"Party pooper."

We munch on our burgers and look out at the ocean. I try to concentrate on my food, but I'm suddenly not very hungry. There are way too many butterflies in my stomach competing for space.

After Kelsey finishes eating, we head out onto the boardwalk where Kurt and the two guys from the earlier Frisbee game are sitting on a nearby ledge. One of them is smoking. I'm relieved to see Kurt isn't, and then wonder why I care.

His face lights up when he sees us. "Hey. Anna, this is Stewart and Jeremy."

The two guys half wave. I point to Kelsey. "This is Kelsey."

"You want to just hang out for a bit? Or go for a walk up near the national park?"

"Actually, we can't…" I start, but Kelsey interrupts. "Let's walk."

Damn that girl. She loves to meddle. I'd forgotten that about her.

She inserts herself between Stewart and Jeremy, threading an arm through each of theirs, and pulling them along the boardwalk. Kurt and I are left there standing alone.

I laugh nervously. "Sorry. Kelsey isn't very subtle."

He smiles. "Don't worry. My friends do that kind of thing to me, too." He nods in their direction. "Are you okay with this?"

"Yes. But I just want to let you know now, I'm already in a

relationship…"

"Anna, I don't expect anything from you. We've only known each other for five seconds, and I didn't even remember the last time we met. I at least owe you my time to rectify that."

Wow. He's good.

"Okay. Thank you. That's very sweet."

We walk slowly up the boardwalk, and I feel tongue-tied. While I was up front about not being available, I still feel a little like I'm betraying Ed.

"I take it you live around here?" he asks.

"Uh, yeah. Just in an estate about ten minutes from here."

"It's a pretty nice area to grow up."

"It is. What about you?"

"I live down in Maroochydore. Not far from the record store, so I can walk to work."

"Convenient."

He looks at me. "You know, I don't think I have met you before, but you seem really familiar. If I believed in reincarnation, I'd say we were friends in a past life."

He's echoing the thought I had at the record store the other day. Of course, in his case, it's sort of true. It makes me wonder if the memory from the other day is cosmically tied to his brain somehow. And if other people are able to do what I'm doing now, it could explain things like déjà vu.

"Sorry, I'm not freaking you out, am I?" he asks when I don't respond.

"Oh, no. You're not freaking me out. I was just contemplating the workings of the universe."

"Do you believe everything happens for a reason?"

"I didn't use to. But I'm starting to question that."

"Me, too."

Kurt and I stop and watch as Kelsey and the boys run down to the water's edge and start splashing at the edge of the waves. It must be freezing.

I shiver at the thought.

"Are you cold?" Kurt asks.

"Um, only a little."

He shrugs off his jacket and drapes it over my shoulders.

"Oh, you don't have to do that," I protest.

"I'm fine. I don't really feel the cold."

I pull the warm fabric around me. It smells faintly of sandalwood, presumably from his aftershave.

"Thank you."

Kurt sits down on the sand, and I join him.

"Tell me about you, Anna."

"What do you want to know?"

"Everything."

I raise an eyebrow at him. "Really? *Everything?*"

"Yep. Do you have any brothers or sisters? Are your parents still together? What's your favourite movie?"

"I have one sister called Amy. Yes, my parents are still together. And my favourite movie…" I have to think back. What movies did I love when I was sixteen? "…is *The Usual Suspects.*"

"Me, too! How awesome is that film?" He looks ridiculously pleased by my choice.

"So good," I agree, silently relieved I didn't say something that hadn't been released yet.

"I'm assuming you're still at school?"

I nod.

"What's your favourite subject?"

"Home economics," I say automatically. "It gets a bad rap because it's not strictly academic, but it's the most practical subject for life after school."

He laughs. "You say that with such conviction."

Because I know it for a fact.

"But it is! You learn to cook, sew, work out a household budget…"

He holds up his hands. "I know, I know. I was just teasing. I did home ec too, and I totally agree. But I have to admit, I only chose it because I thought it would be easier than physics."

"Unless you're going to be a scientist, home ec was probably the better choice."

"You're right." He looks at me, and I almost shiver again, despite not actually being cold. "Tell me about your boyfriend."

I blink. "Why?"

"Because I want to know whether he's worthy of your time."

I laugh. "That's a little possessive of you, but all right. You don't have to worry. He's good to me. He has a good job…" I'm about to say, he supports me, but that's not strictly true. Ed isn't exactly the kind of guy you go to for emotional support. But I've never really needed that. I like to deal with stuff on my own.

"That's it? He's *nice* to you and he has a decent job? Does he show interest in *your* interests?"

I don't like where this conversation is heading. "Please don't assume you know my boyfriend. He's a good person…"

"I'm sorry. I didn't mean to make you feel uncomfortable. I guess I'm just a little jealous, and I want to know what I'd have to do to capture the attention of someone like you."

You've already done more than enough.

"Well, you can remember my face next time," I joke. I know I'm being unfair, but he nods good-naturedly.

"Oh God. I can't believe I don't remember you from the store. Seriously, I must have been hungover or…I don't know…recovering from a lobotomy or something."

I laugh, despite myself.

"Guys!" Kelsey is waving to us. "Come over here!"

I glance at my watch. It's getting late. I don't have much time left.

Kurt tilts his head in Kelsey's direction. "Should we?"

"Probably. Kelsey doesn't take no for an answer."

"I gathered that already."

Kurt stands and holds out his hand to help me up. I pretend I don't see it and jump to my feet. He gives me a bemused smile. "I don't bite, you know."

"I know."

I run down to join Kelsey and the guys. Kurt follows me.

Kelsey is lying on the sand. She pulls me down beside her and points at the sky. "We're arguing about what that star is called," she says.

I follow her finger. "It's probably a planet. Maybe Jupiter?"

Kurt lies down on my other side. "Wow, the stars are bright tonight."

"Can you see the southern cross?" Kelsey asks.

"Of course," I reply.

Kurt leans in close to me and points upwards. "My favourite star is next to Mimosa, which is the left point of the southern cross. Can you see it?"

I look carefully. "I think so."

"It's actually a cluster of stars called the Jewel Box and they're over ten million years old."

"Wow. How do you know this?"

"My grandfather was really into astronomy and he used to show me all this cool stuff with his telescope."

I focus on the sky and think about how the stars look the same in the future. It's comforting.

"The Jewel Box will remind me of you now," Kurt whispers.

I'm about to tease him about bad pick-up lines when I start to feel dizzy. I reach out and grab Kelsey's hand. "It's Cinderella time," I tell her.

She sits up and leans over, brushing my hair away from my face. "Come find me in the future," she says so softly that only I can hear.

I nod, but everything is spinning and there's a chance my head doesn't actually move.

Kurt seems to understand something is going on and he reaches for my hand. I only have a split second to appreciate the warmth of his skin on mine before it fades.

And then everything disappears.

ELEVEN

I wake up in bed in Brisbane. The clock says it's 6am. It's so weird, sleeping all that time and not feeling any different than if I lived a whole day normally and then had a proper night's rest. Does my brain just switch to sleep mode around 8pm? I wonder what would happen if I took the compound at 3am. Would I still sleep all the way through to the next morning even though it would wear off at 3pm?

I rub my eyes and sit up. Am I causing damage to the universe, despite it not affecting my current one? I revisit my original assumptions of how the compound works. At least I can rule out a *Back to the Future* scenario.

I still don't know if I'm hallucinating or dreaming, but I guess for all intents and purposes, it doesn't really matter what I call it. Except, I still don't know whether a) my brain is making up everything as I go along, or b) I'm slipping into the real 1996. And if it's B, where is the other Anna's brain while I inhabit her body? And does everyone in that version of reality go back to the original timeline the next day as Kelsey proposed?

I lean back against my pillows and contemplate yesterday. In particular, last night. It was so lovely hanging out with Kelsey again. And seeing Kurt…the way-too-nice-for-his-own-good Kurt. I know nothing happened between us, but I still feel bad. Probably because when he grabbed for my hand, I didn't want him to let go.

I go out into the kitchen and make myself a cup of tea. It takes a few minutes to readjust to this body and time.

The kettle is still boiling when my phone rings.

Ed.

"Hey!" I say brightly. "How's your trip so far?"

"Busy. I was in meetings all day yesterday, and I have a client breakfast in about ten minutes. Sorry I didn't call last night, but I didn't get back to my room until almost midnight, and I didn't want to disturb you. How are you doing?"

"Not too bad." I don't know how else to reply, because I've done nothing outside of 1996 since he left. And then I think about how sterile our communication has been lately compared to the conversations I've had with Kelsey and Jackson…and Kurt. I flounder around for something meaningful to ask.

"Ed? What was your life like before you met me? I mean, I know you said you hated high school, but tell me something fun that you remember."

"You want to do this now?"

"Yes! Why not?"

"Um, because I just told you I have to be at a client breakfast in ten minutes?"

"So, you won't have *any* time to talk to me while you're away?"

He sighs. "I didn't say that. It's just, I have a lot on my plate right now. Work is ridiculously busy, and I need you to understand that and give me a bit of leeway."

"What does that mean? Would you rather we didn't have any contact until you get home?"

"No, no. But I can't really do the whole deep and meaningful thing first thing in the morning in the middle of a business trip. Sorry."

I feel like there's more to it than that.

"Why don't you like talking about the past?" I push.

He doesn't reply for a moment. "I just don't."

"Were you bullied?"

"No."

"Did you have a bad experience at school or university?"

"No, it was nothing like that. It was just a crappy part of my life that I'd rather forget, okay?"

"Is it because of your mum?"

Silence.

Ed's mum died a year after he finished high school. Obviously, I have always suspected it wouldn't have been a very pleasant time in his life, but that doesn't explain why he doesn't look back fondly on the time before that. His mum died suddenly from a brain aneurism, so there was no warning or suffering beforehand.

"I just finished telling you that I didn't have time for this crap, and now you want to delve into the worst thing that ever happened to me?"

"I'm sorry, Ed. I'm just worried. We've been together for a large part of our adult lives and I still barely know anything about you from before we met. Isn't that weird? You know all about my life."

"But I never asked about yours. You volunteered the information. And to be honest, I didn't want to know the names of all your ex-boyfriends or anyone you had feelings for before me."

I feel like I've been slapped. Ed has never even hinted he was upset about me bringing up my past before now.

"Well, maybe you should have mentioned that at the time."

"Look, I know you've had a marvellous life, pretty much since you came out of the womb, but not all of us were so lucky. It was bad enough the first time. I don't want to have to rehash everything over and over for eternity."

"Fine," I say quietly. I didn't have a 'marvellous' life as he so patronisingly put it, but I'm not going to argue with him when he's acting like this.

"I'll call you again when I get a spare moment. Talk soon."

He hangs up, and I sit there, staring at the wall.

Wow. Okay, then. I guess that conversation is over.

***

All morning, I feel out of sorts. I'd like to think I have thick enough skin to deal with a moody Ed by now, but my whole world has been quite bizarre lately, and I'm not feeling particularly stable.

I work on a new post for my blog, just to ground myself, and then go to the bookshelf and pull out Ed's and my wedding album. I need to be reminded of happier times.

Ed and I met when I was twenty-two and he was twenty-four. It's quite funny, because he grew up around Shell Beach, too, but we didn't meet until a night out in Brisbane after we'd both moved there. I'd already been to France to do my pastry chef training, and I was partway through the dietician course. I know it sounds like a strange combination, but I wanted to first know how to make great-tasting food, and then how to make it healthy. I worked in patisseries for a while, and a few high-end restaurants, but after my blog took off, I decided to pursue that full-time.

The first time I saw Ed was inside the Family nightclub in the Valley. It was at the height of its popularity, with long waiting lines out the front and packed dancefloors on both the ground and third floors. I wasn't friends with Kelsey by that point, so I was out with an acquaintance from the restaurant I worked at.

We were sitting at one of the bars on the third floor when Ed walked over to order a drink. He looked sad, and I felt compelled to make him smile.

"I seem to have lost my phone number. Can I have yours?"

He looked at me, taken aback, and then burst out laughing. "I haven't heard that one before, but it sounds like something my friend Chandler would say."

"I'll bet that Chandler is a smart guy," I teased.

"Yeah, but he's not really my type," he said, eyes twinkling.

"So, is this Chandler out with you tonight? I want to make sure we're not using the same material. That could get a little awkward."

"Nah. He's up at Shell Beach visiting his family this weekend."

"Shell Beach?"

"Yeah. Why?"

"I grew up in Shell Beach!"

He looked at me strangely. "Really?"

"Yeah! I went to Shell Beach State High and graduated in 1997."

"I grew up in Shell Beach, too! Well, for a few years, anyway. We moved around a lot on the coast."

"Did you go to my school?"

"No. My parents sent me to St. Helens."

"Ah. Private school boy."

"And I graduated a couple of years before you."

"How random. Hey, your friend Chandler doesn't happen to have the surname Robinson, does he?"

His jaw dropped. "You know him?"

"A little. I think my sister Amy dated his younger brother for a while."

"That's crazy."

"Yeah, but you know how small Shell Beach is. Everyone knows everyone."

"Still."

After that, we spent the whole night dancing and talking. I can't even remember what happened to the woman from work that I'd gone to the club with.

Ed and I dated for six years before we finally got married. I wasn't in a huge hurry, and Ed always seemed reluctant to fully commit. Not that I ever questioned his feelings towards me. I always just thought it was a guy thing.

And I think back fondly on all those years. Our wedding was low-key, but beautiful. Ed was slightly melancholy on the day, which I assumed was because his mum wasn't there to be a part of it, but otherwise we were happy.

I flick through the pages of the wedding album. We had some of our photos taken on Shell Beach, and one of my favourite shots was of us barefoot with the pinky-purple early evening sky behind us. The ocean was a pretty blue-green, and the sea foam glowed white.

I wonder when this distance set in between us. Maybe it's been going on for a while, but I only noticed once I experienced a different reality.

Either way, I'm going to make things better. I'll try to stay upbeat on the phone each night while Ed is away and then really work at making our relationship strong again when he returns.

I suddenly have a brainwave. I won't be able to see Ed for the rest of the week here in the present, but I could track him down in 1996. If this version of him won't tell me what happened in the past, I'll get the eighteen-year-old version to tell me.

I sort of feel like I'm betraying his trust, but at the same time, I'm intrigued. I want to know what he looked like…how he thought…if he's the same guy I know now but just in a younger body. And I feel like it will bring us closer in the long run if I know where he came from. This will be good for our marriage.

I spend the rest of the day looking through our garage for any hints of Ed's past. I've never snooped before, but I'll need some help if I'm going to have any hope of finding him. He was one of the first students to study at the Sunshine Coast University, enrolling in a business and law degree and going on to do a post-grad course in Brisbane later on.

I trawl through a bunch of unlabelled boxes and those that just have the word *Miscellaneous* written on top. Some are mine—full of old books and school reports. Some are Ed's, but it's only stuff he's collected since we met.

I've almost given up when I stumble across a shoebox I don't think I've seen before. It's tucked away in the corner behind the Christmas tree decorations.

I gently lift it down and open it up.

Jackpot.

I pick up a bunch of old photos and flick through them. They're mostly of Ed and his parents. He's an only child, although he does have a ton of cousins who made sure he was never lonely, especially after his mum died. I had never seen any childhood photos of my husband—something I think is definitely not normal. He was such a cute kid, too. The photos are clearly from the eighties, with Ed wearing tiny little football shorts and tight navy-blue singlets. His hair was styled in a crewcut, and he looked so happy. My heart breaks for the little boy who will lose his mother before he's had a chance to completely grow up.

There aren't many photos from his teens, but I find a couple from a family holiday when he was about fourteen. I wonder why he doesn't have any others. Are they at his dad's? At least I'll know who to look for when I go back.

I'm disappointed that there aren't any letters or paperwork from when he was younger. I'll still have no idea where to find him.

I'm just about to close the box back up when I catch something glinting in the corner. It's a little silver sun-shaped charm, like one from a bracelet.

I turn it over in my hands, but it doesn't give me any clue as to why it's there.

I shrug and put it back in the box, returning everything to its spot behind the Christmas decorations.

I think I'll have an early night. It's going to be a big day tomorrow, and I'm going to need all the energy I can get.

TWELVE

After a quick shower the next morning, I make up a dose of the compound and gulp it down.

I wake up again in my old room with the sun only just peeking over the horizon. I change into my school uniform and pack some regular clothes in my schoolbag. I have no intention of going anywhere near the school gates today, but I'll have to make sure Mum goes out, so she won't be able to answer the phone if the school calls. Dad will be leaving for work soon, and Amy won't notice if I'm not around. We never saw each other during the day, and we certainly never walked to or from school together.

I make sure my mobile phone is charged and throw it in my bag too. I wish I had my iPhone. This *thing* I own in 1996 can only make phone calls and send text messages. It doesn't even have a touch screen, so texting is a nightmare. If I had the internet, email, and GPS, it would be so much easier.

I go downstairs and make myself some breakfast. I'm starving.

As I'm putting some bread in the toaster, Dad appears.

"Hi, sweetie. How did you sleep?"

"Not bad, thanks."

"Do you have a busy week at school?"

"No more than usual, I don't think."

"Are you on track with all your subjects? I was thinking the other day, it's not too late to switch from home ec to physics. I know you're already doing biology and chemistry, but it would look good on your university application if you'd done all three of the sciences."

"You mean for dentistry?" I clarify. I think back to my conversation with Kurt the other night. It's funny how we were talking about these very subjects. "I like what I'm doing now, but I appreciate the suggestion."

"Are you sure? Home ec is such a cop-out."

I take a deep breath. "It's not a cop-out. I don't see why just because something is fun, it should be considered less important. Besides, don't you think you should learn to cook and look after yourself as an adult?"

He laughs. "Of course I do. But you don't need to waste a school subject on it. You figure out that kind of stuff on your own."

I so badly want to tell him I had a huge advantage in my pastry class thanks to the lessons we dedicated to making profiteroles and eclairs in high school home economics.

"Please, Dad. Let me make my own decisions."

"Okay. Sorry. I just want to make sure you're financially secure when you're older."

I sit at the dining table and start to eat. It makes me sad knowing that even if you do all the right things, life still might not work out the way you want it to. I mean, look at Mum getting sick and Dad having to sacrifice his job for her. Mum worked in a department store before Amy and I came along, and had been talking about re-entering the workplace right before she fell ill. But once her energy levels dropped, she was basically housebound.

"Morning, honey." Mum enters the kitchen, tying a bow in her dressing gown belt. "You're not normally up this early."

"I guess I just wanted to get a head start today."

"Good for you. Do you need me to pick you up this afternoon, since you're working at three thirty?"

"Oh. Um, maybe." Damn. I'm working? I guess that will be another thing I disrupt today. I've decided from now on, I'm going to assume this reality continues after I leave, so I hope this version of Anna forgives me if she gets fired for not showing up to her job. I worry that my last visit and the whole fake pregnancy thing will have completely ruined that Anna's life.

"How will you get there otherwise?"

"All right. Thanks, Mum. Yeah, if you don't mind."

I figure I can always phone later and tell her I'm getting a lift with someone else. I won't worry about it now.

Dad gives me a kiss on the cheek. "See you later."

"Bye, Dad."

He gives Mum a kiss, too. They seem more playful now than they do in the future. Which is understandable, but still depressing.

"What are you up to today, Mum?" I ask.

"Not much. I thought I'd just potter around the house. Maybe do a grocery shop later."

I think quickly. "Oh, I just remembered! We're doing a drama thing at school tomorrow and I need a pair of black leggings. If you get a chance, do you think you could go to the shops this morning to buy them for me?"

She frowns. "This morning?"

"Well, it doesn't *have* to be this morning, but I saw on TV that there's a big sale on at The Palace today, so you'd probably avoid the crowds if you went early." I cross my fingers behind my back.

She sighs. "I wish you had given me more notice, but okay."

"Thanks, Mum!"

I feel bad manipulating her, but if I'm going to achieve my objective of finding Ed, I need to avoid a similar situation to last time.

"I want you to walk with Amy to school today," Mum says. "I'm worried she's been cutting class."

I inwardly groan. "I don't want to be your spy."

"You're not spying. I just think she'd be less likely to wander off if you're with her. And if you want me to buy leggings for you, the least you can do is this one thing for me."

"Fine," I sigh. God, I'm starting to revert to my sixteen-year-old self. I wonder if any of my brain chemicals are being corrupted in this body.

"Thank you."

Amy ambles down the stairs. "Did I hear my name?" she asks sleepily.

"I just said it would be nice for my two girls to walk to school together for a change," Mum says.

Amy looks at me, panicked. "But Anna isn't cool, Mum. She'll ruin my image."

"Hey, I'm cooler than you," I retort. And then decide that yes, my brain is definitely corrupted.

"Girls! Do as I ask for once, please."

"Okay," we both grumble.

Amy gives me a death stare. Like it's my fault. And then I think maybe we can both work this situation to our advantage.

As we leave for school, I turn to her.

"All right, so the reason Mum wants us to walk together is because she thinks you're cutting class."

Her eyes widen. "She said that?"

"Yes, and I don't care if it's true or not, because today I have somewhere else to be. If you promise to keep your mouth shut, I won't say anything either. I asked Mum to buy me leggings at The Palace this morning, so she won't be at home if school calls to check up on us."

Amy looks at me with respect. "I might have underestimated you, sis."

"So, you agree to stay quiet?"

"Sure. Where are you going?"

"To find someone."

"Who?"

"Just some guy."

"Ooh—is he your boyfriend?"

"Not quite. But I'm going to go that way." I point away from the school. "And Mum offered to pick me up this afternoon, so I assume she means to get you as well. Just make sure you're at the front gate regardless of what you decide to do today."

She reaches over and gives me a hug. Amy and I never used to hug as teenagers—and I can't remember the last time we hugged as adults.

"Thanks, Anna. You're rad. See you later."

We go our separate ways. I don't know if Amy plans on actually going to school or not, but that's her problem. She ends up turning out all right career-wise, so she must learn enough to get by. In the future, she's an interior designer for a well-known Valley firm, and I've seen enough of her stuff online to know she's quite talented.

I duck into a block of public toilets at a nearby park and change into my casual clothes. Now that I'm free, I have no idea where to start looking for Ed.

I see a phone box and notice it has a phone book inside secured by a piece of rope. I can look up Ed's number! Or at least his parents' number. Ed said he moved a lot, so he could be anywhere on the coast.

The phone book has seen better days, but most of its pages still seem to be intact. I open it up to M and scan through the entries for Matthews. Jeez. There are a lot. Why couldn't he have a less common name? Ed's dad's name is Steven, so I skip to the S listings. There are three. One is in

Maroochydore, one is in Kawana, and one is at Peregian Beach. I dial the one at Peregian Beach since it's the closest. It rings out. The Kawana one turns out to be an old lady called Sandra who has never heard of Ed or his parents. I dial the Maroochydore one, and a message comes on.

"Hi. You've reached the Matthews'. We're not able to come to the phone right now, but if you leave your name and number, we'll be sure to call you back."

It's a lovely sounding woman. Could it be Ed's mum? It's distressing to know that she won't be around for much longer. Ed told me she passed away just before Christmas in 1996.

I figure I can catch a bus to Peregian and check out the first address, and then if Ed doesn't live there, I can continue on to Maroochydore on the next bus. I find the nearest bus stop and wait.

A few minutes later, one arrives, and I climb on. It's almost empty. I sit near the front and rest my hands in my lap.

I look out the window at the glimpses of ocean as the bus takes its meandering journey down the coast. I'm weirdly starting to feel like this is more home than Brisbane. It could just be because I spent a lot of my early life here. I was born in Melbourne, but we moved to Shell Beach when I was five. The most important years of my life occurred around this area.

Or it could just be that because I've never made really good friends in Brisbane, I don't feel like I have the roots.

I wonder if I'll have time to call Kelsey today. It will be interesting to see how she responds to my revelation of her secret if I need to use it. But is there any point in telling her who I really am? I don't know if I have the energy to go through the same scenario all over again.

We get to Peregian, and I jump out. I stupidly forgot to check which street I was after. I again lament the lack of GPS and Google Maps on my phone. I almost laugh when I realise that Google doesn't even exist yet.

What did people do back in the nineties when they were lost? If you were driving, you would use the street directory in your car. But what if you were on foot?

I see a service station up ahead. Maybe their staff will be able to help me. I go inside and buy a bottle of Coke and ask the guy at the counter if he knows where Cormorant Crescent is. He pulls out a map and unfolds it in front of me.

"It's about two kilometres that way," he says, pointing in the direction my bus just came. I sigh. I guess I have all day, so a twenty-five-minute walk shouldn't be too bad. And hopefully I can wave down the next bus at an earlier stop, so I won't have to walk all the way back here after.

"Thank you."

I trek back up the road, sipping my Coke. At least the weather isn't too hot. For a winter's day though, it's quite mild, and the sky is blue. I love being on the coast on days like today.

I finally reach Cormorant Crescent. The house belonging to this S. Matthews is pretty impressive. It's a two-story concrete-rendered house painted white with terracotta trims, and it has a beautifully kept tropical garden out the front. I can't say I even knew whether Ed's family had money when they were younger. His dad lives alone in a small apartment in Shell Beach now.

I nervously go up and ring the doorbell. And then panic. What am I supposed to say? Why didn't I spend some time planning a cover story? For some reason, I keep thinking Ed will automatically know who I am, but of course he won't.

A girl in her early twenties answers the door.

"Yeah?"

"Oh, hi. I was just wondering if Ed lives here?"

"Nope. No Ed here."

"Do you know Ed Matthews?" I ask, not wanting to feel like the last twenty-five minutes have been a waste of time.

"Sorry. I don't."

"Okay. Thanks."

I start to walk away, and someone calls out to the girl from inside the house.

"Just some weirdo looking for an Ed," I hear her yell back.

Hey! That was a bit uncalled for. Oh well. As long as Ed's parents don't have a silent number, I'm pretty sure I have their address now.

I manage to catch the next bus without having to walk too far, and find myself in Maroochydore half an hour later. I should have asked for directions to this address at the last service station, but after a quick visit to another one, I find that the house I'm looking for is only a couple of blocks away.

I'm not far from The Palace, so depending on what happens with Ed, I figure I can grab some lunch there afterwards. Hopefully, Mum will already have bought my leggings and left the mall by then, so the chances of running into her will be slim.

At least not being prepared in Peregian has forced me to think through what I'm going to say now. I'm going to ask to use Ed's phone to call a friend under the pretence I'm lost.

I reach the street I'm after and find the house. It's a little old white bungalow with a green roof. As I walk up the driveway, I note that it's not nearly as fancy as the last place I went to.

There's no answer when I knock, but I can hear faint music coming from around the back.

The driveway continues on to a shed in the backyard, so I follow it around and peek at the source of the noise.

I freeze. Thankfully, there's a tree to hide me, so I position myself behind it.

Ed is there. He's reclining on an old-fashioned sun lounger and smoking a cigarette. I didn't know Ed smoked! He hid that well.

He looks great, though. As an eighteen-year-old, he'd grown out the crewcut and had his hair longer on top so that it covered half his face. I watch as he chats to a girl lying beside him on a towel on the ground. She's flicking through a magazine—and she is absolutely gorgeous. Her hair is long, straight, and brown with natural blonde highlights, and she has lovely, tanned skin. Her toned body is clad in a tiny coral-coloured bikini, and I can tell from here that she has beautiful full lips painted a dark red.

I wonder about their relationship status for a second, until she suddenly jumps up and straddles Ed, leaning forward and kissing him deeply. I experience a sudden rush of conflicting emotions. This is my husband kissing another woman! I'm jealous but intrigued. Who is this girl?

I inch a bit closer to see if I can hear what they're saying.

"Do you have to go to uni?" the girl sighs. "Can't you stay here? I'll make it worth your while." She runs her tongue down his stomach to illustrate her point.

Ed groans. "Oh God. What are you doing to me? You know I have an exam this afternoon! If it was any other day, I wouldn't go." He points to a book beside him. "I should be studying now."

She pouts. "What time do you finish? Can I stay here and wait for you?"

"If you like. I'm sure Mum won't mind. You know she loves you."

"She's the best," the girl agrees.

I feel an additional stab of envy that this girl got to have a relationship with my husband's mother—and an apparently mutually favourable one, too.

"Now, baby, I really should finish off this chapter." He pulls her in for another long kiss and then playfully pushes her off the lounger. "Stop distracting me."

She crawls back over to the towel and unties her bikini top, tossing it on the ground and lying facing up.

I feel like an intruder, but I can't look away. Ed glances at her and throws up his hands.

"Come on! You're playing dirty now."

He leaps up and launches himself on top of the girl, kissing her exposed breasts and rubbing his hands all over her body.

I can't take anymore. I back away as quietly as I can. Except I didn't count on knocking over a pot plant. Shit.

The ceramic pot shatters on the ground, but I don't stop, bolting down the road without looking back. I hide in a neighbouring yard and pray that no one is coming after me.

And then I start to cry.

THIRTEEN

I'm not sure how long I cower in that stranger's front yard, but I'm glad they don't seem to be home. I know I'm being totally irrational. After all, I should have expected this. Of course Ed has a past. Just because he's never told me about it, doesn't mean it never existed. And this was when I was sixteen! I had just broken up with Todd, so I can't talk.

But what he seemed to have there was way more serious than my stupid high school fling. And she was so pretty! And confident! Ed was always going on about how I needed to be more outgoing. Was he thinking about this girl when he said it?

I wonder how many other girlfriends he had between her and me. It could be dozens. Or it could just be her. Ed was eighteen in 1996. He could technically have dated her for another six years before I came along.

I finally stretch out my legs and walk off in the direction of The Palace. I check my reflection in the side mirror of a nearby parked car and see that my eyes are puffy, and my skin is all pink. I didn't even bring my sunglasses with me. I can't go to the mall looking like this.

And then I spot the perfect location for brooding. An internet café. The interior is dark and almost deserted. I go to the counter and pay for a computer, sitting right in the corner, as far away from the door as possible.

I stare at the bulky PC and monitor on the desk in front of me.

What am I supposed to do now?

I half-heartedly log on, and an AltaVista search box appears on the screen. I have no idea what to type. The news sites didn't even properly exist back then. All I remember doing is sending emails and chatting to US college boys online.

Interestingly, I still have the same Hotmail address I had at sixteen. The realisation makes me laugh as I type in the email's web address. What password would I have used in 1996? I had a habit of using celebrity crush names, but I don't know who I would have been into at the time.

And then I remember the spine of my diary. John! I type in John, plus my favourite number, which is thirteen. My first attempt with everything in lower-case doesn't work, but the second one with a capital J logs me in. I feel like I've just won the lottery.

I have lots of emails from Kelsey, and a bunch from the aforementioned college boys. Jeez. Some of them were intense! One guy called Lex declared his love for me, and I never even knew what he looked like. Did I just shrug it off as a joke? Another one was trying to arrange a time so we could chat more intimately. Ew. I guess the internet always had the potential for exploitation.

I skim through the messages from Kelsey. I'd forgotten that we used to write to each other at lunchtime in the computer lab, even though we were practically sitting next to each other in the same room. I think we were just obsessed with the novelty of the internet at the time.

I stop at one message with the subject *Are you OK?*

Hey babe,

How are you coping post break-up? I know you're the one who did the dumping, but I also know a big part of that decision was because of what Todd did to you at the party. That was really sucky of him. Don't worry, we'll find you another guy soon. Someone way hotter than that idiot Todd!

I start to cry again. Right now, the guy who is supposed to be a million times better than any other guy I've ever dated is making out with someone else. Even in the future, things are weird between us.

I try not to make any noise, but a small whimper escapes.

"Are you okay?"

You've got to be kidding me. Is this the universe's idea of a joke?

I turn around and come face to face with Kurt.

"I'm fine," I mutter. This is the last thing I need…Kurt being nice to me when I'm in the midst of a marital crisis.

He kneels down beside me. "Are you sure?" He glances up at the computer screen. "Are you upset because of what it says in that message?"

I snort. "No. Todd was a tool."

"Oh, okay. Do you want to talk about what *is* upsetting you?"

"Not really." I should get up and leave. He's not going to remember anything after today anyway, so it won't matter if I'm rude.

He doesn't get the hint. "Do you want to come and get a drink? I'm on my break, and it will be much more interesting if I have company."

"What are you doing here?" I sniff. "Don't you work at the music store?"

He doesn't seem surprised that I know this. But then of course anyone could have visited and seen him there. "Yeah, but it's only around the corner and I was going to kill some time with this lame computer game before I have to go back." He holds up a CD with a creepy looking cover and the title *The 11th Hour*.

I have a vague recollection of Todd talking about that game.

"Is that the sequel to *The 7th Guest*?" I ask, despite myself.

His eyes light up. "Yes! You know it?"

"Sort of. I haven't played it or anything. I just know some people who have."

He grins and looks outside. "That's cool. But you know what? I've decided it's too nice a day to spend indoors. Come and hang out with me."

I hesitate. I shouldn't. I really shouldn't.

He sees me wavering. "Come on. It's not every day I meet a girl who has actually heard of the computer games I play."

"Or who can tell the difference between vinyl and CD," I joke.

He looks even more pleased. "Yes! Oh my God, you get it!"

"Someone showed me the difference recently, and I finally understand the fuss."

"Well, then you definitely have to come and hang out."

I battle internally for another few seconds and then shrug. Why not? This man keeps being thrown in my face. I might as well get to know a bit more about him. I can be a mature adult about it.

I stand up. "Lead the way."

We walk back out onto the street and Kurt ducks into a small takeaway shop to buy a couple of bottles of lemon squash.

"What if I didn't like lemon squash?" I ask, half smiling as he hands me the bottle.

"I just had a feeling you did. And if you didn't want it, I'd just keep it for myself for later. Oh, but before we go any further, I have to ask you one question. Do you like sarsaparilla?"

I wrinkle my nose. "No. That stuff is disgusting."

He laughs. "Good answer. I don't think I could spend time with anyone who likes sarsaparilla."

We walk down a side street that leads to the water. There's a picnic bench right at the edge. He sits down and pats the space beside him. I join him, but make sure I don't get too close.

"I'm Kurt, by the way."

I almost say, "I know," but catch myself in time.

"Anna."

"It's nice to meet you, Anna." He opens his drink and takes a long sip. "So, what brings you to this part of town today?"

"I…uh…was sort of looking for someone."

"And it didn't go well, I take it?"

"Not exactly."

"I'm sorry to hear that. You live around here?"

"Um, no. I live at Shell Beach."

"Oh, cool. I have some cousins who live up that way. Rachel and Chris Morgan."

I feel my eyes widen. "Seriously?"

"Yeah. Why?"

"Rachel's one of my good friends!"

"No way! That's trippy."

"So, how come I've never seen you before?" I'm wondering if this somehow explains the familiar feeling we've both experienced. Maybe we've seen each other without officially meeting.

"I'm sort of banned from going to their house because their dad doesn't like me. He thinks I'm a bad influence."

"Why?"

"I took Chris to see Metallica without his permission a few years ago."

"Oops."

"Yeah, but it wasn't a big deal. At least from my perspective."

"So, you didn't get in any trouble then?" I feel like there must be more to the story.

"Well, Chris did go home with a nose ring that he didn't have before he left the house, but that's not a big deal."

I laugh. "Really?"

118

"I suppose it *is* kind of weird. It's not like there was a piercing place at the gig, so he must have had some random stranger do it. But he's fine. He didn't get hepatitis or anything. As far as I know."

I can't tell if Kurt is making this all up or not. He's smiling, so that could mean he's either recalling a fond memory or pulling my leg.

I don't say anything for a minute, so Kurt fills the silence.

"Hey, shouldn't you be in school today or something?"

"I told you before. I was looking for someone."

"A guy?"

"Naturally."

"He's a fool if he can't treat a pretty girl like you with respect."

I almost say that he's called me pretty twice now, except he hasn't really. At least not in this version of reality.

"It's a bit more complicated than that."

"Whatever it is, just know that nothing is ever as bad as it seems at the time. Especially in high school."

I clench my jaw. "Thank you, oh wise one. You're all of, what, twenty-one?" I know he's just trying to help, and I know Chris said something similar at Rachel's party, but this is completely different. This is my future husband. And also, I'm upset as a thirty-something, not a sixteen-year-old.

He holds his hands up in surrender. "Sorry, I didn't mean to offend you. I was trying to make you feel better."

"Well, don't. You have no idea what I've been through or what my situation is, so please don't patronise me with talk of it all being insignificant just because I'm sixteen."

"I apologise. I shouldn't have belittled your feelings without knowing anything about you. And for the record, I'm twenty-three."

"Still a baby then," I tease, trying to lighten the mood.

"What does that make you then? An embryo?" he retorts.

"Maybe. I probably know more than you think." I'm playing with fire, but I'm enjoying this banter too much to shut it down.

"All right," he says. "What do you think of politics?"

"Australian politics?"

"Yep." His mouth twitches.

Damn. I knew Bill Clinton was the president of the US in 1996, but only because Kelsey reminded me the other day, and also because I was so obsessed with the presidential campaign in 2016. I have no idea about Australian politics around the same time.

"Who's the prime minister again?" I joke.

"I knew it. You talk a good game, but you can't even give me an opinion on John Howard."

Oh. Wow. Was John Howard the prime minister that far back? Okay.

"Actually, I think he's going to stay in power for a long time," I pretend to speculate. "And I think he's going to have quite an impact on the country. A lot of people will respect him, but when he finally gets kicked out, it will be a huge defeat. He will do a couple of good things…" I pause when I realise that the Port Arthur Massacre has only just happened. "…like tighten up gun laws…but I think overall, he will cause a fair bit of damage."

Kurt stares at me open-mouthed. "That's very specific."

"I told you. You have no idea what's going on in here." I tap my brain in illustration.

He looks sheepish. "I was actually just stirring you. I can't stand politics. I haven't even enrolled to vote yet."

"What?" I slap his arm playfully. "So, you're trying to make me feel all uneducated while you're even less so?"

"Not caring about politics doesn't make me uneducated. But I guess I deserved that."

"You totally did."

At that moment, I somehow drop my bottle of lemon squash. Fortunately, it doesn't smash, but its contents start leaking out over the ground. Kurt quickly rests his own bottle beside him on the bench, and we both lean forward at the same time to pick it up. Our hands brush, and I quickly pull my fingers away from his, because it felt like I might catch alight if I maintained contact. As we both sit up again, our faces are only a couple of inches from each other. Kurt is holding my bottle in one hand, but he reaches out to stroke my cheek with the other.

I jump up and pick up my backpack. "I have to go. Thanks for the drink."

He looks surprised. "Do you want to take what's left?"

"No, thanks." I start walking away. "It was nice meeting you."

"Come and visit me at the record store sometime?" he calls out after me.

"Maybe," I call back, knowing full well that's not going to happen.

I can't even risk a look back.

Kurt is not part of the plan.

Ever.

FOURTEEN

I head over to The Palace and enter the food court. The events of the morning have completely messed me up, and I'm hoping some lunch will make me feel a little more normal. As I inspect what's on offer, I lament the absence of Grill'd and Roll'd and all the other fancy fast-food places we have in the future. In 1996, my choices include a carvery, a Red Rooster, and the Chinese and kebab stalls I saw when I came here with Mum the other day. They don't even have sushi! This food court has two sushi places in the future.

I decide on a plate of noodles from the Chinese buffet and take it upstairs to the seating area away from the crowds.

And almost drop my tray when I see Ed's girlfriend sitting alone in the corner.

She looks up briefly, but then goes back to reading a book. She has a white sundress and denim jacket over her bikini now. Up close, she is even more stunning. Damn her.

I sit at the table next to her and begin eating. I want to find out more about her, but I don't know what to say.

After a couple of false starts, I take a peek at the cover of her book. It's *The Celestine Prophecy*. I remember reading that in the late nineties. Wasn't a big part of its message synchronicity? I'd say running into this woman is a pretty good example of that.

"I love that book," I say, pointing to it.

She looks up. "You've read it?" She seems surprised.

"Yeah. It really made sense to me. You know, opening yourself up to new experiences and stumbling upon coincidences."

Her eyes light up. "I know! It totally works, doesn't it?"

I had thought I had outgrown new-age superstition years ago, but obviously in my current situation, I can't claim to know anything. There have to be other forces at work out there. "I think so."

"Like how I met my boyfriend, Ed. We just kept running into each other randomly over and over. I swear it was at least five times before we realised the universe was trying to tell us something. So, we finally talked, and it felt like we'd known each other forever—even though we'd had completely different lives up to that point."

Huh. Ed is the most logical person I know and always makes fun of things like fate and serendipity. Could it be because of his experience with this woman?

"That's really sweet. How long have you been together?"

"For over a year now. I never thought I would be one of those people who settled down with someone right out of school, but I feel like Ed is my soulmate. We've already talked about getting married, and he's made jokes about how he would propose."

"Oh?" I start to feel uncomfortable. This isn't the Ed I know at all. I was proposed to during an episode of *Seinfeld,* and I almost missed it because he said it so casually. A wave of jealousy crashes over me. How come this woman got a better version of my husband than I did?

"Yeah, he said he might hire a sky writer and take me up to a lookout…or whisk me away for a special weekend in a fancy hotel and put the ring in a glass of champagne…" A dreamy smile comes over her face.

"He sounds very romantic."

"He is." And then she looks at me. "Sorry, I've been rambling on about myself. So, what kind of stuff have you experienced as a result of synchronicity?"

I frown. I can't exactly say that I was just spying on her at my future husband's house and then found her here. That would be very stalkerish, even if it was an accidental discovery.

"Um…I guess I…oh! I went to Thailand with my family last year, and I ran into a girl on Patong Beach who I hadn't seen since we were in primary school together, and it turned out we were staying in the same hotel in rooms opposite each other!" This actually did happen when I was a teenager.

"That's really cool!" she says. "Hey, what's your name?"

"Anna."

"I'm Maddie." She holds out a hand for me to shake. I feel weird touching her. Like I'm violating something between Ed and I.

And then I notice the bracelet on her wrist. A charm bracelet.

"That's cute," I say.

"Oh, yeah. Ed gave it to me. He buys me a new charm every time he wants to remember something we did or somewhere we went."

My heart turns to stone. Ed has never been sentimental towards me. Ever.

"Do you mind if I take a look at it?"

"Sure." She turns her wrist slowly so I can see the different charms. There's a heart, a key, a lock, a star, a music note, a pineapple…and a sun-shaped charm. The exact same one I found in the shoebox at home.

"I like that one," I say, pointing to it.

"Oh, yeah. That's my favourite, too. Ed got that for me after we stayed at Byron Bay one weekend and watched the sunrise from Mount Warning."

I feel like my throat has closed up. "That's really sweet," I choke out.

She gently pulls her wrist away and closes her book. "Sorry, I have to go. Ed is at uni, but we're going to the movies to see *Mission Impossible* afterwards, and I need to go pretty myself up for him."

I smile at her. I wish I didn't like her, but I do. "It was nice meeting you."

"You, too. Maybe synchronicity will mean we run into each other randomly in the future."

"We might."

She leaves, and I look down at my now cold Chinese food.

I've lost my appetite.

***

I wander aimlessly around The Palace for a couple of hours feeling restless and confused. Is this all as big a deal as I'm making it out to be? I know I had some pretty intense relationships at the end of high school—some that burned hot and fast and then faded within a month or two. But Maddie said they'd already been together for a year. And seeing them earlier made it look like Ed was just as dedicated to her as she was to him.

And the charms. Why would he keep that sun charm all these years unless he wanted to remember the memories associated with it?

I don't know why I thought tracking down Ed in the past would be a positive thing. I guess part of me thought he'd had a big falling out with a buddy or something, and I could comfort him. I certainly didn't expect to find something like this.

What does it all mean? Does Ed never talk about Maddie because he still has feelings for her? And if so, are they stronger for her than they are for me?

I'm dragged out of my moment of self-pity by a loud beep on my phone. A missed call. I mustn't have heard the ringtone in time. I dial in to messages and listen to Kelsey's voice.

"Hey, where are you? Why aren't you at school? Call me at home after three thirty or just come over if you're not sick."

At least I have my best friend. I'm starting to think our friendship is the only good thing about revisiting 1996.

And sure, meeting Kurt has been interesting, but he just confuses the whole situation. I like him, but after our last interaction, I can't see him again. It wouldn't be fair to Ed.

I stay at The Palace until just before school finishes, and then catch the bus straight to Kelsey's house. She's already home. Andy is nowhere to be seen, thank God.

I let myself in and find Kelsey in the kitchen making herself a glass of milk and some cookies.

"You want some?" she asks.

"No, thanks. I'm not hungry."

"So, what happened to you today? You're obviously not sick, and it's unlike you to stay home on a school day."

"I had some stuff to do."

"You don't look so great. What were you doing?"

"I was down at Maroochydore looking for someone."

She stares at me. "Who? Why am I only hearing about this now?"

"It's kind of a weird situation, but it didn't work out, so it's not worth talking about."

"I want to know, though. Tell me!"

"Just some guy I met randomly, but I found out he has a girlfriend."

"Where did you meet him?"

"Down at the river," I lie.

"You're so weird. You just started talking to some stranger at the river and then decided to stalk him all the way to Maroochydore?"

"Something like that."

She shakes her head. "Okaaay…you're obviously completely over Todd, then?"

"Of course I'm over Todd. He forced himself on me. We broke up."

"He was asking about you today."

"Was he now?"

"Yeah. He wanted to know where you were and if you were all right."

I wrinkle my brow. I don't remember ever talking to Todd again after we broke up. Could one day of absence make him reconsider his feelings towards me? Not that I care. He was rude and borderline rapey. I don't want anything more to do with him.

"Oh well. Maybe he realised how badly he behaved, and if so, good."

She takes a gulp of her milk and nibbles on a cookie. "So, I'm trying to work out how we can see Aaron again."

I groan. "You're not still obsessed with him, are you?"

"Not obsessed. In love. There's a difference."

"Is that right?"

"Yes, we're going to get married one day, and I will have his babies."

"Good luck with that. I don't know why you're so interested in a guy who doesn't pay you any attention."

"Because he hasn't gotten to know me properly yet! Once he finds out how charming I can be, he'll be falling all over himself."

I laugh. "You *are* charming, but I think you can do better than Aaron."

"Like who?"

"I don't know. There are lots of other guys out there. Ones at other schools…and after next year the whole world will open up. If you move to Brisbane, you'll have heaps to choose from."

"But I want Aaron," she whines.

I wish I knew what her future held apart from the two losers she dated after we finished school. I'd love to tell her that she settled down with a respectable guy who adored her, but I have no idea what she's up to.

"I'm sure someone else will come along soon who you'll like just as much."

"I doubt it." She changes the subject. "So, does your Mum know you didn't go to school?"

"No. I don't think she'll find out. I made her go out this morning, so if the school rang, she wouldn't have been able to answer the call."

Kelsey looks impressed. "Sneaky."

"You'd be surprised what I'm capable of."

She laughs but then turns serious for a moment. "Just be careful, hey? You don't want to mess up your life for a guy. Whoever this one was you were looking for today—he's not worth the heartache. Take your own advice. Someone better will come along who you like just as much."

I almost burst into tears. I don't want to think that's possible. I want Ed. I want everything to be back to normal, before I knew what happened in his past.

But how do you erase a memory? I can go back in time, but I can't get rid of the knowledge.

I shiver.

This whole time travel thing is now kind of a nightmare.

FIFTEEN

I end up leaving Kelsey's house before the compound wears off and head down to the river. My phone rings, but when I see it's home, I ignore it. And then I remember I was supposed to work this afternoon. Oops. That's definitely not going to happen now. I quickly text Mum, saying I got a lift with someone else and that I'll call later. I don't want her to call the police and report me as a missing person or anything.

I switch off my phone and sit down on the edge of the sand, slightly shaded by a tree. I feel so helpless, stuck here in 1996. I want to talk to future Ed and get reassurance that we're fine.

At least I only have to wait for an hour.

Around 6pm, I start to feel drowsy. I lie down, using my bag as a pillow and hope that if there is another Anna who takes over after I leave, she isn't too freaked out about waking up here.

Back in the present, I feel more lost and lonely than ever. I sit up in bed and look around at the room. It's always been just as much my space as Ed's, and I can feel his overwhelming presence everywhere I look. His clothes hanging over a nearby chair…the scent of his hair product lingering on the pillow next to me…the ghost of what I thought were happy memories, but which now feel slightly tainted.

My phone is lying next to me on the bedside table. I've had no missed calls.

I dial Ed's number. He shouldn't have left for work yet, but it just rings out and goes to messages.

Damn him. Why can't he be who he led me to believe? I always thought my husband was a quiet person, someone who considered things seriously and never tolerated silliness. But now I know that he used to be light-hearted and fun. Was it his mum's passing that changed that? Or something that happened with Maddie? I wish I knew.

I go out into the study and sit in front of my computer. I don't know why, though. Ed doesn't believe in social media. He doesn't have a Facebook account, and he isn't even registered on LinkedIn, which is unusual for someone who works in a corporate office in the city.

It's not like I can see if he's friends with Maddie online. I look through my own friend list on Facebook and see if there's anyone who would have known Ed back when he was a teenager.

It's a shame I'm not closer with his dad. We got along pretty well in the beginning, but over the last few years, Ed has distanced himself from him, because his dad has a bit of a drinking problem. As a result, I have also had less contact. It wouldn't feel right calling him out of the blue. Or would it?

And then I see a guy called Ty in my list. I remember that he went to school with Ed. I'd unfollowed him a long time ago due to his prolific posting about Isagenix supplements. We only became Facebook friends in the first place because he was getting married and wanted to get in touch with Ed to invite him to a boys' weekend.

I gingerly open his profile, ready to face the onslaught of spammy marketing posts. Ugh. Yep. He's still at it.

Is it worth risking being promoted to?

Yes, it is. This is my marriage in crisis. I need to have all the information if I'm going to make any major decisions about my future.

I reluctantly send him a private message.

Hey, Ty. I know this is kind of random, but do you remember any of Ed's ex-girlfriends?

He doesn't answer immediately, so I pace around. I don't have much housework to do and I'm not hungry, so I flick on the TV and half pay attention to a cooking show. I normally like watching that kind of stuff, but today I don't find any enjoyment in it.

This is ridiculous. My life was good before. Why did I have to go and mess with it?

After almost twenty minutes, I hear my laptop beep. I cover the ground between where I am and the study in one flying leap.

My heart races as I read the reply.

LOL. Why?

I'm going to have to come up with a plausible excuse. Um…

Me: *I have some weird chick messaging me on Facebook who claims she knew Ed in high school and wants to catch up on old times. I just wanted to know what I'm letting myself in for before I agree.*

Ty: *Oh my God! That's hilarious. OK, I only knew of one real girlfriend. Her name was Maddie.*

There it is. Proof that she's a real person and not a figment of my imagination.

Me: *And what was her last name?*

Ty: *Mcfeeley. I only know because we used to make jokes about it. So, is it her?*

I roll my eyes. This guy is a class act.

Me: *Oh! Ed just got home. Sorry, I have to go! Thanks for the info!*

Ty: *No worries. Say hi for me.*

Me: *Will do. Bye.*

I let out a deep breath between pursed lips. I guess that means I am *literally* travelling back in time.

I shiver.

Now that I have Maddie's name, do I want to take this any further? I hope Ty doesn't contact Ed to let him know I've been digging into his past. Maybe I should have gone back to 1996 and asked someone there instead.

But I'm starting to wonder if I should use the compound again at all. It's brought me nothing but heartache so far. And now that I know everything is real…

I type Maddie's name into Google and click on Images. No one that looks like her comes up. Maybe it's short for Madison.

A quick search disproves that theory.

Hmm. Maybe Madeline?

Bullseye.

I know it's her straight away, even twenty years on. She's like Will Smith and doesn't seem to have aged at all. In fact, I think she looks even better now.

My hands shake as I click on her photo and follow the link to the website it belongs to.

It's a fancy media agency. Maddie is the CEO.

I know immediately Ed would love that. He likes that I cook, because it means he doesn't have to, but he has never really respected my job. I think he secretly thinks it's unfair I make money from doing something I enjoy.

My heart sinks as I read her bio. There's not a single thing on there that would make me think Ed wouldn't be impressed.

I write her an email, mentioning that I might be interested in rebranding my website to attract more readers. I'm not sure what I'm trying to achieve, but I need to do something.

Just before I shut down my email program, I notice a new message from my supplement company.

> *Hi Anna,*
>
> *We are happy to hear you received our latest batch of supplements and hope you are able to use them in one of your fantastic recipes. However, we are a little confused as to what you mean by 'youth compound.' We don't have a product by that name and hope you haven't opened it yet. We advise that you send it back immediately so we can look into its origin for you.*
>
> *Please let us know if you have any further questions.*
>
> *Regards,*
>
> *Pam – Marketing.*

I don't know what to do with this information. They don't know what it is? What if the compound was doing some sort of long-term damage to my brain? I could end up like those people who have bad acid trips and turn partially psychotic for the rest of their lives.

Except I don't feel any after-effects from taking it. It kind of worked exactly as advertised. And it did have the company's logo on it, which makes it even weirder. I suspect Pam in marketing might not know every product in their range.

That has to be it.

At least that's what I'm going to tell myself.

Any other option is too frightening to contemplate.

***

Ed doesn't call me back all day. Normally, I would be a little put out that he's too busy to phone his wife, especially after our last conversation, but part of me needs some time to process and think about what I'm going to do next. If Maddie gets in touch tomorrow, I might arrange to meet her. I don't know what I would say, but I always have the excuse of talking about my business. I guess I'll just wing the other stuff.

I sleep restlessly and dream about 1996 again. But this time, I know it really is a dream. Everything is disjointed, and I see flashes of Kelsey and a young Ed down at Shell Beach. Ed's face morphs into Kurt's, and I wake up feeling guilty.

I feel like I should spend some time out and about in the present day, reminding myself that I have an actual life outside of my husband and work—but just as I'm contemplating a trip into the city, my phone beeps with an email notification.

It's Maddie.

Hi Anna!

Thank you so much for getting in touch! I've followed your work for a couple of years now and I absolutely love your recipes! I would be honoured if we could meet to discuss some tweaks to your branding. You're already doing really well, so I wouldn't change anything too dramatically. As it happens, I have an hour free around ten if you want to meet for coffee? I'm a little obsessed with Jocelyn's on James Street. Let me know if you can make it.

Maddie.

I gulp. Okay. I know I could just ignore her invitation, but I feel like I'm on a trajectory I have to see out. I won't be able to relax until I get the full story.

I quickly write a reply, thanking her for making time at short notice, and tell her I'll meet her in a few hours.

This is really happening.

***

I feel slightly ill as I near Jocelyn's Patisserie. This is the final chance for me to back out and pretend like nothing ever happened. But of course, it's already too late for that. I know things I can't unlearn, and I need to hear it all.

I take a deep breath and push open the door to the café.

I look around. She's there, sitting at a small table in the corner. We make eye contact, and she smiles. I sit down opposite her.

"Hi, Maddie. I'm Anna."

"I figured," she says, gently teasing. I don't want to like her, but I do. She has a quiet confidence and charisma that I can imagine would make her quite popular. "Would you like a coffee? I was just about to order one."

"Oh, no, let me. What would you like?"

She stands up. "Don't be silly. You're the potential client. It's on me."

"Uh, then maybe a double shot espresso?"

She laughs. "A woman after my own heart. I'll be back in a sec."

I watch her head over to the counter and order our drinks. I know this probably won't end well, but it's like a scab I can't leave alone.

Maddie returns and puts the two coffees down on the table. "So, you're looking to rebrand?"

"Uh, yeah. As you said in your message, I'm doing okay already, but I haven't revamped my image for a few years, and I read somewhere it's good to do that."

"Well, only if your existing branding isn't working. Say, if you wanted to reach a different audience or reposition yourself with a different focus, then you should do it. But despite being the CEO of a media agency, I'm a big believer in not fixing something that isn't broken. With that said, how are your web visitor figures? Are they increasing? Decreasing? Stagnating?"

"I guess I get about a dozen new followers on Instagram each week. My web traffic is pretty stable. I have decent interaction on Facebook."

"Good." She opens a notebook and starts writing notes. "And you have a sponsor, so I guess they provide the majority of your income?"

"That's right."

"They've never expressed any displeasure with their ROI?"

"No. I send them a report each month with all the stats. They seem happy."

"What about your book? How's that going?"

"Wow, you really do know my business," I say, smiling.

"That's my job. To be honest, I usually delegate these kinds of meetings to my account managers, but I've always liked your stuff and wanted to meet you personally."

Damn it. She's too nice for her own good.

"That's very sweet of you to say. Well, to answer your question, the book is doing all right. It's through a publisher, so they take care of everything and send me a royalty cheque every few months."

"Have you ever thought of indie publishing?"

"Not really. I wouldn't know where to start."

"I have a guy in the office who knows the ins and outs of Amazon. If you're interested, I can introduce you to him and you can have a chat. It might be a good way of developing further passive income. And you'll be able to keep more of the profits. You already have a huge fan base, so the bit that most people find difficult is already done."

"Sounds good."

She takes a sip of her coffee. "As for your website, I don't know if you need to do much. Maybe tweak the colour scheme a little? Metallics and pinks are in at the moment. Also, maybe add in an identifying mark that you can carry across all your marketing? You don't really have a logo, so it will help more people remember you if you have an icon of some sort."

"That's a good idea. I take it you have a guy who can help me with that, too?"

"Sure do."

"Thank you."

I hadn't actually expected to take the business side of this meeting seriously, but I quite like her ideas.

"I bet you work long hours as a CEO," I say.

"I probably do. But I don't notice anymore. I love my work." She doodles on her notebook. "My husband used to hate it, though."

Here's my chance. "Used to?"

She sighs. "We split up about five years ago." She then covers her mouth with a hand. "Sorry, I don't know how we ended up talking about my personal life. Ignore me."

"No, no. That's totally fine. I'm sorry to hear about your marriage."

"It's okay. It was a long time coming. He wanted to start a family, but I wasn't ready."

"Ah. Yeah, my husband and I don't want kids either."

"Oh, I do want them, but there was something stopping me then. I suppose if I'm being honest with myself, it was that I wasn't ready to have kids with *him*. I know we were married, but sharing a child seemed more final. Like our lives would be linked forever if I got pregnant, even if we split up." She laughs. "Wow. I never talk like this to my clients. Do people ever tell you you're really easy to open up to?"

I chuckle. "Sometimes."

"I guess I feel like I already know you from following your blog."

And I already know you from meeting you in 1996.

"I like that," I say honestly.

My heart starts racing. This is it.

"The reason you didn't want kids...was there...someone else? Feel free to not answer me if it's too personal," I say, half-joking.

She's quiet for a second.

"Not in an affair kind of way, no. But yes, there was someone who seemed to overshadow my relationship with my husband." She suddenly focuses on me with laser-beam accuracy. "Do you feel like your husband is the best man you've ever been with?"

Until recently I would have said yes without hesitation. But after finding out what I have...

"I do," I say, deciding I don't need to complicate things. I'm glad I retained my maiden name for business purposes so Maddie won't be able to make the connection between me and Ed.

"See, you're lucky. I feel like I messed up. Or the universe messed up. I met my soulmate just after high school." Her eyes glaze over. "He was so sweet. It felt like we were especially made for each other. I don't know if it was teenage hormones or not having the weight of the world on our shoulders, but life was so easy and fun. I know that sounds silly and I'm sure everyone has a first love they look back on fondly, but I really thought I would end up with mine."

"What happened?"

Her face goes dark. "His mum died. I wanted to support him and make sure he was okay, but he shut me out. I knew he was hurting, so I gave him space when he needed it, but I also tried to stop him from falling into that void."

"You couldn't?"

She shakes her head slowly. "We didn't break up right away, but it wasn't the same after. He started drinking heavily and getting into fights with people whenever we went out. He never seemed to notice I was even in his presence. In the end, he broke up with me. I told him to take some time to sort out his head and that I would wait, but he insisted we cut ties permanently. I think he was trying to protect me, rather than himself."

"I'm so sorry."

She looks at me again. "I always wondered what happened to him. I tried looking him up on Facebook, but he doesn't have a profile. I couldn't even find him on LinkedIn or anywhere else online."

"Some people don't like social media," I say.

My husband is one of them.

"Yeah, but it makes it difficult to get closure, you know? If I found out he was happily married with a bunch of cute kids, then I could move on. But not knowing…"

This is the moment where I tell her everything. Only I can't.

"You never know what the future holds," I say. "You might meet someone else just as good."

"I don't think so," she says, resigned. "I guess I just have to be happy with the memories. Some people never find that kind of love. At least I had it for a short while."

I suddenly feel awkward. I sip my coffee and wait for Maddie to collect herself.

After a moment, she becomes business-like again. "Anyway, we should get back to the reason you're here." She rummages around in her purse and hands me a tasteful business card in light blue and grey. "Here are my details. I'll talk to the guys in the office, and we'll come up with a proposal for you. But feel free to contact us in the meantime if you have any ideas you want us to consider."

"Thank you. I really appreciate you meeting me here."

"No. Thank *you*."

I stand up and half wave as I try to exit the café as naturally as possible.

It's only after I'm outside and have walked up the street and turned the corner into a narrow alley that I start to hyperventilate.

I don't think I wanted to know any of that after all.

SIXTEEN

For the rest of the day, it's as if I'm in limbo. Ed and I need to have a serious talk when he gets home.

He finally arrives just after 7pm. I've made him his favourite dinner, which is mushroom risotto, and I've poured him a glass of white wine so we can start the evening off as gently as possible. Especially considering we haven't spoken since Tuesday morning when we argued.

He comes through the door holding a bunch of lilies. His expression is suitably apologetic, but I don't know if it's because he knew he was being harsh when we last spoke, or because he hasn't been in touch since.

"I'm sorry, babe," he says, handing me the flowers and leaning in to kiss the top of my head.

"For what exactly?" I say lightly.

"For not calling. I know I should have, but I never seemed to have more than a couple of minutes to spare, and by the time I got back to my room each evening, it was really late, and I didn't want to inflict the tired version of me on you."

"You know I wouldn't have minded."

"But *I* would. I thought it'd be best if we just started over when I got home. Forgive me?"

"Of course."

He loosens his tie. "Something smells good."

"I made your favourite."

"I'm a lucky guy."

"You are," I laugh.

"I'll just get changed and then we'll eat, okay?"

"Sure."

I watch Ed walk into our room and feel strangely disconnected from everything. It's like I'm playing a role now. The devoted wife. Is Ed doing the same? The dutiful husband?

I serve out the risotto and sit down to wait for him.

He reappears and sits opposite me, immediately digging in. I watch him, trying to gather clues about what's really going on in that brain of his.

"Ed?"

"Hmm?"

"Do you have any regrets?"

He stops eating for a second and looks at me properly. "About what?"

"The past and the choices you've made…"

He doesn't say anything for a moment and takes a sip of wine.

"Everything turned out the way it was supposed to, so no, I don't think I have any regrets."

"What if something wasn't resolved the way you thought it was?"

"What kind of something?" He says it slowly, like he's being backed into a corner.

Okay. However he reacts to what I say next will determine our future. I'm not sure I realised the gravity of the situation until now. I almost don't want to go there, but I have to. If I don't, I would forever be wondering, and it would destroy us anyway.

I take a deep breath.

"Maddie. What if the situation with Maddie wasn't resolved?"

His eyes widen, and his face clouds over with a mixture of wariness and fear.

"How do you know about Maddie?" he asks, barely above a whisper.

There's my answer. I feel all the air go out of my lungs. If he didn't care about her, he wouldn't have answered that way. My first instinct is to shut it down and pretend it's all a joke. But I know it can't happen that way. I have to face this head-on.

"I met her the other day. And I know she was your first true love. And you were hers."

Ed now looks pained. "Anna, why are you doing this? How did you even meet her?"

I can't tell him the truth. "It was a weird fluke. I ran into her at a café in New Farm. She recognised me from my blog, and we got to talking about my business. She offered to put together a marketing proposal to help me maximise exposure."

"And how on earth did you find out she was my Maddie?"

The way he says *my Maddie* breaks my heart.

"I don't know. Women talk about stuff. She was musing about what life would have been like if her first love's mother hadn't died when he was eighteen. I was about to say that my husband had also lost his mother at eighteen, but when she said your name, I knew we were talking about the same person."

"And?"

I want to cry at the poorly hidden look of hope in his eyes.

"I didn't tell her who I was."

His shoulders slump, and I know that isn't the answer he was hoping for. I wonder if it's because he was hoping I would have done his dirty work for him and told her he was taken.

"Do you want to tell me about her?" I ask.

He shrugs. "There's not much to tell."

He's such a bad liar. "There obviously is, Ed." I take a second deep breath and pull the card out of my pocket, placing it down on the table in front of him. "This is her number. You should call her."

He looks at the card like it might bite him. I can see how scared he is of this sudden twist his life has taken.

"But I thought you didn't tell her…"

"I didn't tell her I was your wife. But she did want me as a client."

I can tell he hates that he's having this conversation with me, of all people. I know he has a million questions but can't ask them.

"Did she seem…" He stops to clear his throat. "…I mean…do you think she wanted me to contact her?"

And with that one question, I know our marriage is in big trouble. As soon as he sees her, he'll be gone to me. I'm not sure how I feel about it. I could have withheld the information, but from the minute I saw her back as a teenager at Ed's house, I knew everything was going to change. I should have taken some more time to psychologically prepare, but I knew if I left it too long, I'd chicken out and I'd never know. Better to rip the Band-Aid off now than let the wound fester underneath.

I shut down all emotion in my brain and attempt to think logically. This is the way it has to happen.

"Probably. And just so you have all the information going in, she's divorced. No kids."

I have never seen Ed look so sick, yet so hopeful in his entire life.

"Why would you tell me all of this?"

"Because you need to sort it out. Your life should not be consumed with regret. Whatever happens between you and I, at least it will be on an even playing field now."

***

I thought I was happy. I thought all marriages were like the one I had with

Ed. It never occurred to me that we were any different. But now that I think about it, I can see we were only together out of convenience, at least on his part. I did love him, but I'm not sure he ever loved me, and that's a very hard thing to accept. We never really argued, because he just didn't care enough. What I mistook for a quiet personality was actually a miserable one…one that had lost all hope when he and Maddie broke up.

"I'm going to go and stay with a friend for a while," I tell him. "I think you need some space to think everything through."

His eyes well up. I have never seen Ed cry, and it feels like my already shattered heart is being pulverised by large steel-capped boots.

I hurry over and wrap my arms around his shoulders, kissing him on the cheek.

"I'll call you in a few days."

"Anna…" he says weakly. I know he wants to stop me, but he also can't prevent this crazy force now that it's begun. I don't think I realised the true power of love until now.

I have to let this happen.

SEVENTEEN

I have basically been a zombie for three weeks now. I drag myself out of bed every now and again to half-heartedly upload a recipe to my blog, but I have zero enthusiasm. And the problem with working for yourself at home is that there's no one to call you out if you're being lazy or don't feel like doing anything.

I haven't heard from Ed since the third day after our confrontation, when he texted to see how I was, and I let slip that I was staying at an apartment I rented through Airbnb. I had led him to believe I would be at a friend's house, but I didn't actually have any friends in Brisbane I could handle seeing right now. When he found out, he insisted I move back in and told me he'd go stay at a place his work kept for interstate clients.

I now don't know if he's waiting for me to make the first move, or whether he's so wrapped up in his reconciliation with Maddie that he hasn't given me a second thought.

I have to find out. I owe it to our relationship. I was so used to our lives running smoothly (even if it was because Ed's mind was elsewhere) that it's quite an adjustment to be experiencing this level of uncertainty. I don't know what to do, how to feel or how to act.

I send him a text, rather than actually call. I don't think I could handle hearing HER in the background.

Hey...how's things? Just wanted to check in...

I have no idea what else to say, so I click *Send*. The ball's in his court now.

He messages back almost immediately, which is reassuring.

Hi. Things are OK. You?

Damn him. Why can't he give me anything to work with?

Me: *Fine. Are you coping?*

Ed: *Sort of. You want to catch up for a coffee or something?*

Me: *Yes! How about our usual at Bulimba?*

Ed: *Sounds good. When?*

Me: *I don't know. This afternoon?*

Ed: *Cool. I can be there at 4.*

Me: *See you then.*

I start to cry. That whole exchange seemed so clinical…like two strangers talking. Well, apart from the fact that I didn't have to remind him of our 'usual' café. But it still isn't how it should be.

I go back to bed for another hour and stare at the ceiling until my eyes hurt.

At three fifteen, I drag myself into the shower and have the water cool in an attempt to freshen up my puffy face.

After bathing, I rub some tinted moisturiser into my skin and add a bit of mascara to my lashes. It helps me look slightly less like a character from *The Walking Dead*.

I pull on a pair of mint-green jeans with a black top and survey the result. Good enough. I'm not going to be mistaken for a supermodel by any stretch of the imagination, but I look passable.

Ed is already at our coffee shop when I arrive. I wonder if we should have chosen somewhere less familiar to have our first catch-up since…I don't even know what to call it yet. I struggle to hold in the tears as I shakily sit down.

Ed offers a tentative smile. "You look nice."

"Thank you. You look like hell."

I don't mean to sound so harsh, but he does. His face is pale, he has big dark circles under his eyes, and it looks like he's lost weight since I last saw him. I wish I was the kind of person who got skinny during an emotional trauma, but I tend to comfort eat, so if anything, I get fatter.

He chuckles. "You always know exactly what to say."

"Sorry. I'm feeling a little unstable today."

"That makes two of us."

"Are you hungry?" I ask.

"Uh, not really. But I could grab a coffee. I haven't been sleeping very well."

"I'll get them." I start to stand up.

"No, no. You stay there. I'll get them."

He doesn't even ask me what I want. Of course he knows I'll have a double shot espresso. My heart aches knowing that if we divorce it will be a long time before I have this level of familiarity with someone else. And then I remember that Maddie also drinks double shot espressos. I cynically think how easy it will be for Ed to adjust to his new life.

He returns a couple of minutes later and puts the drinks on the table. I open my purse to give him some cash, but he waves me away.

"Don't be silly. It's only a few dollars."

"I know. But I don't know what you're thinking or expecting."

"I'm not thinking or expecting anything."

"I guess we should talk about..." I can't even bring myself to say her name out loud. It would make it more real and final somehow.

He sighs. "I guess we should."

"Have you seen her much?"

He looks pained and doesn't respond for a moment.

"Ed. We have to be honest with each other from now on. There has been way too much secrecy in our relationship from day one. It's time to tell me everything now."

He rubs a hand through his hair. "Yes. I've seen her. Twice."

I know I instigated this whole thing, but it still kills me to hear it confirmed. And the fact that it's been more than once makes it worse.

"And?"

"We've talked."

"What about?"

"Just catching up on stuff—finding out what the other has been doing since we last saw each other."

I almost don't want to ask, but the words are out of my mouth before I can stop them.

"Have you…?"

He knows what I'm getting at and cuts in so I don't have to finish the question.

"No! Nothing like that. I promise. We're married. I wouldn't do that to you."

I feel like he leaves off the end of the sentence…*until we were officially over.*

"So, have you talked about what happens next?" I prod.

"Not really. I wanted to get everything straight in my head first."

"How's that going?"

His eyes bore into mine. "I don't know, Anna. You're the one who turned our lives upside down. Were you unhappy with me? Did you not think our marriage was working?"

I feel like I've been slapped. "Hey! Don't put this all on me! You're the one who couldn't wait to go and see Maddie the second you knew how to reach her. But now that you bring it up, I *do* think our marriage left a lot to be desired. You work so much that we barely ever see each other. We never kiss properly. And I can't even remember the last time we had sex."

I realise I'm talking a little too loudly, but I don't care.

Ed looks around, embarrassed. "Would you keep your voice down? You're making a scene."

"Oh, you couldn't bear for that to happen, could you? You have to have everything perfect all the time, according to your rules. You know what? I didn't want to go to Prague. I wanted to go to Hawaii! And I wanted to organise it myself, not have it delegated to some woman I've never met. And for the record, my job is important to me, and I wish you respected it more!"

His eyebrows shoot up into his hairline. "So, what, you've just had all of this simmering away for however many years and didn't think to say anything?"

"Would it have made a difference? You've been emotionally closed off because of Maddie. I just didn't realise until I met her."

He lets out a frustrated growl. "It wasn't all because of Maddie. And I told you not to mess with the past. I still don't know how you even found her."

I contemplate telling him about the Youth Compound, but I know how that would go down.

"I told you. I ran into her at the patisserie in New Farm."

All the fight suddenly seems to go out of him and his shoulders slump.

"What do you want, Anna?"

"I want a husband who doesn't think of me as second prize."

"I'm sorry if you felt that way. It was never my intention."

No, but it's the truth. And you didn't disagree with my statement.

I take a deep breath. "I think maybe I'm going to see a lawyer. You should probably do the same."

"Is that what you want?" he asks. "A divorce?"

"Of course I don't want a fucking divorce, Ed! But I also don't want to stay married to someone who clearly wants to be with someone else." I wish I could point out that he bought a charm bracelet for Maddie to celebrate every important moment in their lives, and I practically had to remind him when it was my birthday. I'm only realising now that our relationship never reached its potential because Ed used up the best of himself with someone else.

He looks at the ground. "Okay. I'll do whatever you want me to do."

I screech in protest. "Why do you have to be so damn passive about all of this? This is why we're here in the first place! You pushed Maddie away, and then because I was the path of least resistance, you ended up with me and miserable!"

"That's not true," he whispers. "I chose you on purpose. And I do love you."

"But not as much as Maddie."

He doesn't say anything.

I swallow down the bile rising in my throat. "If we go ahead with a divorce, I'll split everything however you like—as long as I have enough money to rent my own place for a while."

He nods. We sit there in silence for a few minutes, sipping our drinks. Then Ed suddenly stands up and comes over to give me a hug. He squeezes me tight and rests his chin on my head. I refuse to cry.

"You are amazing, Anna. I'm sorry to put you through this."

I close my eyes and commit this moment to memory. It's probably one of the only genuine moments of our entire relationship. I want to remember how Ed smelt, how he felt and how *I* felt in the last seconds of our marriage.

After a few seconds, I gently pull away. "I think I'm going to get my drink to go."

He nods. I approach the counter and ask them to put my coffee in a takeaway cup. I then walk to the door of the café, turning one last time to make eye contact with Ed.

He definitely doesn't look happy, but there is a tiny trace of relief on his face.

I guess this is how it's supposed to be.

***

When I get home, I sink into a deep despair. I've always found it weird that grief isn't linear. Some moments, I feel at peace, and others I just want to curl up in a ball on the floor and never move again. And it sucks that I don't have any good friends in Brisbane. Why don't I have any good friends in Brisbane? Actually, I can't think of any good friends I have elsewhere either. When did this happen? Did I just get wrapped up in my job and rely on fans to keep me company online?

I miss Kelsey, but right now I don't have the energy to track her down and go through all the drama of a reconciliation. I couldn't bear having her reject me.

I wonder...

No! That damn compound is what got me into all this trouble in the first place. Nothing good has come of it. Maybe the right thing happened as a result, but definitely nothing that has made my life better.

I get the jar out of the cupboard and look at it. It's still almost full. I sit down on the couch and put it on the coffee table in front of me.

I won't do anything hasty this afternoon. But if I still feel this way tomorrow, I might use it.

Maybe.

EIGHTEEN

I sleep badly—as I have done ever since Ed left. When I finally decide to get up and stay awake around 5am, I'm feeling more miserable and exhausted than ever.

I still crave Kelsey's easy company, so I make the decision to go back to 1996. I think it will be good to have a break from the bleakness of my current reality, even if the compound is the reason for it in the first place.

I eat a light breakfast and then mix up a dose. I don't even notice the taste anymore. I brace myself for what's to come and lie down on my bed.

It's just after six when I wake up in my old room. I'm lucky it's the weekend, so I don't have to worry about coming up with a way to avoid school. I don't know if I'm supposed to be working, but that wouldn't be until later in the day anyway.

I get up and dress in a pair of jeans with embroidered flowers down the side and a form-fitting top with a zip in the middle. I pack a bag with my phone and wallet and sneak downstairs, leaving a note for Mum and Dad that says I'm going to the beach for the morning.

I then catch a cab over to Kelsey's and climb up to her balcony, knocking on the glass. I hear movement inside, and after a second, I see her eyes peeking around the side of the curtain. When she sees me, she yanks it back and slides open the door.

"Anna! What the hell are you doing? You scared me half to death!"

"Sorry. I wanted to talk to you, and I didn't think your mum would appreciate me calling your home phone so early. You need to get yourself a mobile."

"Pfft. How am I supposed to afford a mobile, huh? I barely make anything at the bakery, and I have to give half of my pay to Mum for board."

"Oh." I forgot that in the past, mobile phones were actually quite pricey to buy and operate. I guess I was lucky my parents wanted to keep tabs on me and bought me mine. I'd also forgotten that Kelsey worked at a bakery. It's interesting that I was the one who went on to be a pastry chef.

"Anyway, what was so urgent that you had to come over at…" She squints at her watch. "…6:35am?"

"I was wondering if you wanted to go out for the day?"

"Um, I guess? What did you have in mind?"

"I don't know. Maybe the Gold Coast or something?"

"Really? You want to go all the way down there?"

"Why not? We could go to one of the theme parks or just hang out at the beach where we don't know anyone."

"Okay! Let's do it!" She seems to warm to the idea quite quickly. I always liked that about Kelsey.

I wait on the driveway while she packs a bag. It doesn't even seem weird that I prefer the company of a teenager to an adult right now.

She meets me outside, and we head to the bus stop.

"You know it's going to take half the day just to get there?" she says.

"I know. But does it matter?"

"I suppose not." She throws her head back and lets the morning sun shine on her face. "God. I can't wait until the end of next year. We could do this kind of thing all the time and not have to answer to anyone."

"Yeah, but then you'll have uni and work—and they're worse."

"Don't say that. Why would you say that and ruin my daydream? Besides, you don't know what it's going to be like. It might be heaps better."

I try to think back to when I first finished school. That summer was a blast, with Kelsey and I going out at least five nights a week. She didn't start studying until February, and I was just working part-time until then, because I didn't want to jump straight into full-time at the video store until the holidays were over. But then we did get a bit busy, and it wasn't as great as I thought it would be.

My time in France—well, that's another story. I want to tell Kelsey all about it...how the country was amazing...how I can now speak fluent French...and how my cooking skills are pretty damn good, even if I do say so myself. I wonder how she'd react if I started showing off.

A bus pulls up. It takes us down to Nambour so we can catch the train to Southport, and then another bus takes us on to Surfers Paradise. I know Kelsey already pointed it out, but I do start to wonder at the intelligence of wasting half the day on a bus.

The journey is pleasant, though. I appreciate having nothing to do other than sit and gossip idly with my best friend. Sometimes she says things that betray her age, but for the most part, she's pretty mature for a sixteen-year-old. Or maybe I'm just immature for someone in their late thirties.

But once we see the Cavill Mall and I feel the electric energy of the Gold Coast, I know the trip was worth it.

We go down to the beach, and Kelsey gets out her coconut tanning oil. Do they even make that stuff anymore? I don't mean the 30+ or 50+ stuff that smells all coconutty, but the actual tanning oil that only has SPF4 or something. I feel like I should warn Kelsey about melanoma, but I know she'll just ignore me.

"I'm so glad we're doing this," she says, sighing contentedly.

"Me too. I really needed today. I don't think I've ever said how much I appreciate you, Kelsey."

"Aw…I care about you too, babe."

I lie there, feeling all warm and fuzzy.

After we get our fill of sun, we wander along the Cavill Avenue strip and stop in all the cheesy souvenir shops. This area goes through a major redevelopment over the next twenty years, even more than Main Street at Shell Beach.

We're just combing through the shelves of a novelty store when I hear a familiar voice. It's not as deep as I'm used to, but it's definitely one I recognise.

I peek around a rack of naughty greeting cards blocking my vision, and my mouth drops open.

No way.

Ed is here? How can Ed be here? Maybe I have no free will, and the universe is just making me think I do.

I glance around to see if he's with anyone, but he appears to be alone.

I grab Kelsey's arm. "I know that guy."

She squints in his direction. "Who is he? I don't think I've seen him before."

"Oh, um, I think he's from Shell Beach."

"Really? That's pretty weird." She skips over to him before I can stop her. "Hey, are you from Shell Beach?"

He looks up, surprised. "Uh, yeah. I mean, I live in Maroochydore now, but my parents used to have a house there. Why?"

"We are, too! My friend Anna here thought she recognised you." She points to me, still half hiding behind the greeting cards.

"Cool." He goes back to reading the back of a box of what I think might be edible underwear. Surely that can't be right. Ed was never that kinky.

"So, do you work up there, too?" she asks, apparently not noticing his lack of interest.

"Um, yeah. I work at the Sheraton restaurant."

I blink. Ed never told me that. The Sheraton is next door to Beans. I was literally only a few metres away from him most days.

My curiosity gets the better of me and I approach him. "What do you do at the Sheraton?" I ask.

He focuses on me but doesn't seem particularly impressed with what he sees. "I'm a kitchen hand. Just part-time while I study business."

"So, you don't want to be a chef or anything?" I push.

"Oh, actually, I kind of do. But law pays better, so I'm going to do that instead."

He then returns to inspecting the box in his hands, not even questioning why a random stranger would be interested in his life.

I can't believe Ed wanted to be a chef! How can he have implied my job wasn't worthy when it was something he once thought he might do? I spent years in restaurants, and he never once relayed any stories about his own experience. That's weird, isn't it? Unless he regrets doing law and was always jealous I made a decent career from cooking?

Kelsey gently touches my arm and nods to the door. I follow her out.

Once we're out of earshot she rolls her eyes. "What a dick."

"Why do you say that? You didn't think he was cute?"

"He was okay-looking, but not very friendly. Here we are, miles from Shell Beach, and he doesn't even try to make an effort when two pretty girls from his hometown try to make conversation?"

"Maybe he was on a mission."

"To buy edible underwear? Yeah, a very important mission."

"So that *was* edible underwear?"

"Yep. I pity the woman who has to deal with *that*."

I can't help but take her comment personally, even if he's with Maddie at this point in time. But when I think about it, I do feel a little sorry for me. At least the sixteen-year-old version. She has no idea she will waste some of her best years on a guy who thinks of her as a runner-up.

I start marching up the street. "You're right. Let's forget about him. I want some food."

***

We're back on the train by mid-afternoon. I've decided to make a stop at Maroochydore before I go home.

At Nambour, Kelsey and I hug and go our separate ways. She heads off to find a bus stop to Shell Beach, while I locate one for Maroochydore.

I do a double-take when I see Ed already lined up in the queue for mine. He must have caught the same train.

"I promise I'm not stalking you," I joke as I stand behind him.

He half turns and looks at me. "Ha. Funny."

It doesn't sound like he thinks it's funny.

I watch as he gets out a CD Discman from his backpack. I can't help myself. "What are you listening to?"

"Oh, just some Guns n Roses." He then deliberately turns away and shoves a pair of headphones over his ears.

Okay. This is definitely all wrong. Firstly, Ed has never *ever* played Guns n Roses at home. In fact, whenever I played anything remotely close to rock, he used to complain. Secondly, why is he being so rude? Right now, he's in a happy relationship, and his mum is still alive. He should have no excuse to act like this.

I'm starting to wonder if the quiet, introverted Ed I loved was actually a selfish bastard all along. I could have mistook what was actually not caring for thoughtfulness.

We get on the bus and I sit as far away from him as possible, which happens to be the front. I don't want him thinking I'm trying to impress him. That is now the last thing on my mind.

When we get to Maroochydore, I climb off without looking back. I stomp down the road, still fuming over Ed's behaviour, both in the past and future.

I'm so busy formulating insults in my head I should have delivered earlier that I don't notice when I almost crash straight into someone on the path.

"Oh, I'm so sorry," I say, jumping back just in time.

"That's okay. I didn't really want that sandwich anyway," a voice says teasingly.

I look up and my heart starts beating a million miles a minute. Kurt. Of course. Because the universe is definitely fucking with me now.

"You."

He crinkles his eyebrows. "Yes, it's me. Ta-da?"

I quickly shake my head, remembering he doesn't know who I am.

"I mean, sorry. Did you say something about a sandwich?"

He holds up a paper bag that I only just noticed was wedged under his arm. "I squished it when I thought we were going to collide."

"Oh. Can I buy you another one?" I start rummaging around in my purse for some cash.

He gently places a hand on my arm and the warmth seeps into my skin, making its way throughout my whole body. "Don't be silly. A little flat food never hurt anyone. But if you're not doing anything, you could come and hang out with me while I eat? Make it up to me with witty conversation?"

I'm torn. I could really use a friendly face after what happened with Ed just now, but I already had plans before he came along.

"Uh, I kind of have to be somewhere before five. But maybe later?"

He beams and holds out a hand for me to shake. "Deal."

"Do you always confirm social plans with a handshake?" I laugh, taking it.

"No, but I am with you."

I look down as Kurt entwines his fingers with mine. Normally I would find an interaction like this with an apparent stranger a little creepy, but it works. It really does feel like he knows me as well as I know him. He gives my hand a gentle squeeze and then pulls away. "I live just down the road. Do you want to call me when you're done with your plans and we can go grab some dinner or something?"

"Again, I need to ask. Do you do this kind of thing with everyone?"

"Only with pretty girls who I feel I've met before."

"I really hope that isn't a line. Because it's terrible."

His face goes serious for a moment. "I promise it wasn't a line."

"Okay." I get out my mobile phone and open the contacts. "What's your number?"

He takes my phone off me and types into it. "Here," he says, handing it back. He then looks stricken.

"What?" I ask.

"I don't even know your name."

"Anna. And you're Kurt." I point to his music store name badge before he can question how I know.

"Well, I'll be waiting for your call, Anna."

I walk away, smiling again, thanks to this beautiful man who reminds me that life isn't all sadness and secrets.

***

It's already 4pm when I arrive at the retirement village, and I'm warned by the staff that I'll have to leave soon. Hopefully, that will be enough time to have a proper chat. But maybe not that much time to see Kurt afterwards.

It's nice to visit Grandma Millie on my own. I didn't do that nearly enough when she was actually alive. I used to just tag along with Mum, even when I was old enough to drive myself.

I find her sitting in an armchair in the corner of the recreation room. There's a big screen mounted on the wall, but the volume is almost too low to hear.

"Hey, Grandma," I say, walking over and giving her a peck on the cheek. I manage not to lose it this time.

"Oh, Anna! What a lovely surprise! What brings you here on the weekend?"

"I just wanted to see you. Find out how you've been."

She smiles. "I'm the same as always."

"And you're feeling well?"

She laughs. "As well as can be expected for someone stuck in a retirement home at age eighty."

I settle myself into a nearby chair. I've never talked to her about getting old before. Our family doesn't really discuss stuff like that.

"Are you scared of death?" I blurt out.

She looks at me, surprised. "No, dear. But what brought this on?"

"I've just been questioning life a lot lately and trying to figure out what the point is."

She looks thoughtful for a second. "You know, I don't think there actually is a point. You need to make your own meaning and do what makes you content. I think being happy is overrated, but if you're content or doing something that gives you purpose, then you won't be upset when

160

you're my age."

"Do you have any regrets?"

She shakes her head adamantly. "Not a single one. Sure, I did some stupid things when I was younger, but nothing that had any lasting ill effects. I see everything as a learning opportunity—even mistakes and getting old." She levels her gaze at me. "You're a bit young to be having regrets."

If only she knew.

"I wish I *didn't* have any regrets, but I committed to something I think maybe I shouldn't have."

I've been mulling over the fact that I might have been deceiving myself for quite some time…hung up on a concept of what the perfect life was. I had my fancy blogging job and the amazing-on-paper husband who cared for me, but he didn't love me. There was no passion. How I managed to live through all those years without admitting that to myself just shows how deep in denial I was.

"Honey, you're sixteen. You have your whole life ahead of you. Learn from this and do better next time. And even if you were my age, there's still time to change." She leans forward and whispers in my ear. "Do you know I've started a little flirtation with the man across the hall?"

I try to hide my shock, but don't do a very good job of it. "Really?"

"Yep. He's a lovely gentleman called Noel. His wife died over thirty years ago, and he never met anyone else."

"So, what does this…relationship entail?" I ask, trying to wrap my head around what she's saying.

She seems to know what I'm thinking and waves a dismissive hand at me.

"No, nothing like that!" she laughs. "His heart couldn't take it! It's all very harmless. But we connect on a level that I haven't been able to do with anyone else for a long time."

"What about Grandad?"

"Well, that was a long time ago now, too. And we definitely had some great conversations, but there's something about Noel. I feel as if we've always known each other. There are topics I would never have dreamed of raising with your grandfather. I was always quite interested in meditation, but if I ever brought up the topic, he would shake his head and tell me it was a bunch of hippie crap. But Noel and I often talk about it and how we incorporate active presence into our day-to-day existence. He even introduced me to some interesting Buddhist philosophy."

I beam. My grandmother would have fit right in with the mindfulness movement in the future. "That's so great, Grandma. I've always loved visiting you, but today is my favourite afternoon of all."

"You're a smart girl. You'll figure it all out. And don't forget that there isn't just one person who can make you feel alive. I think the statistics are much kinder than that. So, don't be miserable your whole life and think you're stuck, or not going to find a better situation down the track, because you will. And every time you doubt it, think of me and Noel."

I chuckle, already picturing them sitting on the two-seater couch, holding hands and quietly enjoying each other's company.

"Thanks, Grandma. This conversation was exactly what I needed today."

"Anytime, dear. Anytime."

I think about the fact that I can't visit her in my older body and start to tear up. "You don't realise how much influence you have on my life."

She reaches out and pats my hand. "That's a lovely thing to say."

"I'm serious. I'm going to study cooking when I finish school and learn how to make amazing desserts, just like you."

Now it's Grandma's turn to tear up. "That's the best news I've heard in weeks. How do your parents feel about it? I thought they wanted you to study dentistry."

"Like you said, I have to find my own purpose. And cooking makes me happy."

"Perfect. You'll have to come and bake for me one day."

"I would be honoured!"

She looks at me earnestly. "I know you'll be a fantastic cook."

I glance at my watch and reluctantly stand up. "I have to go, but it was really good seeing you today. Thank you."

"Anytime. And just remember, it's never too late to change something that doesn't work in your life."

"I *will* remember that."

I leave her, feeling grateful that we got to have such a positive conversation. I've become even more inspired by the woman who already influenced my life so heavily.

She definitely deserves to be the role model she is.

NINETEEN

Despite Grandma Millie's words of encouragement, I'm unsure whether I should be pursuing an evening out with Kurt. Besides the fact that I have less than an hour until I pass out, I didn't come back to 1996 to find him. Except here he is, thrust in my face again. I never used to believe in fate, but I'm starting to now.

I get out my phone to call him, vowing not to let things get out of hand. This is just me spending some time with a nice guy in what is still essentially a dream.

He answers immediately. "City Morgue. How may we dispose of your loved one?"

I snort. "So classy."

"Is that the delightful Anna?"

"It is," I confirm.

"I'm so glad you called. Are you done with your appointment?"

He says it in such a way that I know he's dying to find out where I've been. "Yes. I was visiting my grandma."

"Aw, that's so sweet. Well, now that you're done, did you want to meet me at Sizzler?"

I laugh. "*Sizzler?* You really know how to make a girl feel special."

"Hey, it's Maroochydore on a Sunday afternoon. We don't have a lot of choice here."

164

"Okay. I'll start walking now. See you soon."

I walk the few minutes to Sizzler and find Kurt already there. There is a long line out the front, something I forgot was common with this franchise in the eighties and nineties.

He looks genuinely happy to see me. Which is weird, considering we only met briefly in this reality less than two hours ago.

"Hey! I wasn't sure if you were going to get cold feet and chicken out," he says.

"Never. I would have told you up front if I was going to cancel."

"That's good. I hate it when people play games."

"Me, too."

He points up at the menu mounted on the wall. "We should figure out what we want to order. Are you hungry?"

"I am, actually."

"I think I might get some seafood. You want steak?"

I wrinkle my nose. "No, thanks. I'm not a steak fan. The seafood sounds good."

He beams. "None of my friends like seafood."

"Now one of them does."

"Is that what we are, Anna? Friends?" His eyes twinkle.

"I hope we can be."

"Good. Me, too."

We order our food at the counter and sit down. A waiter brings us a slice of cheesy pan bread each and we eat that before talking further.

"So, Anna. What made you take up an invite from a random stranger on the side of the road?"

"Well, for a start, you're not random. I've seen you at the record store before."

"Really? I'm sure I would have remembered if I'd seen you."

"What if you were out the back proving to someone that vinyl was better than CDs?"

He laughs. "I don't do that!"

"Are you sure?"

"I promise you I have never done that in my life. Although, I might make an exception for you."

"And what would you play for me?"

He leans back in his chair and thinks for a moment. "Probably something by Bob Dylan."

"*Sad-Eyed Lady of the Lowlands?*" I ask.

His mouth drops open. "I would totally play that song for you. How did you know?"

"Lucky guess," I say enigmatically.

"That's not a lucky guess. That's reading my brain. You're not psychic, are you?"

I wonder how far I can push it. "I might be."

"All right. Tell me something else about me."

"Um…you hate sarsaparilla?"

He roars with laughter. "I do. But so do most people."

"You…you're named after Kurt Vonnegut."

"I am! But then apart from Cobain, there aren't many other Kurts around. And I was already born by the time he got famous. I'm impressed, though. Okay, tell me something else."

"You're a closet nerd. I bet you like games like *The 7th Guest* and *The 11th Hour.*"

"Well, that's just getting creepy now. I think you actually might be psychic. All right, my turn. How about I try to guess a bit about you?"

"Sure. Go ahead."

He studies me for a moment.

"You're kind. Nice to your friends."

I blush.

"You're very observant."

"Pfft. I think I just proved that to you. That doesn't require any psychic ability."

"You love your family."

"As you would have deduced from me visiting my grandma just now."

"You're beautiful."

My face feels even hotter. "Again, not something you predict. But I do appreciate you saying so."

"And I feel like our lives are going to be intertwined for some time to come. Longer than you realise."

I look away. I wish that were true. But I'm not so sure.

"I'm not freaking you out, am I?" he says, suddenly looking worried.

"No. I'm just thinking about whether that might actually be the case."

"It will be if I have anything to do with it."

Actually, it's probably more up to me.

Our food arrives—a massive platter of fried fish, calamari, and chips. I contemplate going over to the salad bar, because that would be the sensible thing to do, except I remember I'm in my sixteen-year-old body. And even if this was reality, there are basically zero consequences from eating a big pile of fried food at this age.

I'd been having such a nice time that I totally forgot I'm about to pass out.

"What time is it?" I ask, panicking.

He glances at his watch. "A couple of minutes to six. Why?"

I jump up and go around to his side of the table. I kneel down and pull his face to mine, planting a gentle kiss on his mouth. His lips are warm and soft—and they feel right. More right than I could possibly ever have expected.

After I pull away, I smile at him. "Thank you."

He looks bemused. "What for?"

"Just for reminding me that there are caring people out there."

He pulls me in for another kiss. "I want to thank *you* then, for reminding me it's possible to feel this way."

I close my eyes and enjoy my last moments with this man. My brain starts to spin.

Here we go.

TWENTY

I don't feel as guilty about that kiss as I should. Maybe it's because it wasn't in the real world. Or maybe it's because I'm still mad at Ed for a) wanting Maddie more than me, and b) being kind of an ass in 1996. I suspect the real reason is because I know my marriage is already over, but that's still a little hard to admit.

I spend the following week living on autopilot. I refuse to take any more of the compound, because I know it's not going to help my mental state—and I don't want to be tempted to track down Kurt, especially since I inadvertently memorised his phone number when he put it in my phone. The fact that he probably exists somewhere in the present has obviously occurred to me, but I'm not even going to go there. I'm definitely not ready to pursue another relationship, and I also don't want to be disappointed by what might be a boring, attached, or even dead Kurt in my own time.

Ed and I haven't communicated again, and I'm not sure what that means. From my end, I'm just waiting for him to show some sort of initiative, since I've been the one driving it all so far. I need him to take over and let me know what he's planning. Getting a divorce is kind of a forgone conclusion, but he has to keep me in the loop.

By Friday, I am going round the twist. The house feels so empty on my own, and it keeps reminding me of our marriage. Around lunchtime, I text my mum and tell her I'm coming to stay for the weekend.

She writes back straight away.

Sure, honey. See you soon! Is Ed coming, too?

No, just me. Ed's busy at the moment.

Which is true. Busy with his true love.

I pack a bag with a few changes of clothes, along with my laptop so I can still do a bit of work if I need to, and embark upon the almost two-hour drive up to Shell Beach.

I haven't done this for ages. As I get past the outskirts of Brisbane and cruise up the highway, I begin to relax a little. It will be good to spend some time with Mum and Dad.

I resist the urge to turn off near Maroochydore and go hunting for Kurt. This isn't my weird dream state of 1996 where he just appears at every turn. I didn't bring the youth compound with me either. I've decided I need to stay in the present at least until everything is finalised with Ed, and even then, I'm not sure I'll use it again. There's not much to be gained from re-visiting the past, except for indulging a silly crush that the other person isn't capable of returning in any meaningful way.

I reach Shell Beach just after lunch. I almost drive to Mum and Dad's old place—the one I've been visiting in 1996—until I remember their current apartment in Noosaville. I continue on up the road a bit further. Both my parents are at home.

"This is a lovely surprise," Mum says embracing me at the front door. She looks a little more lively than last time I saw her in this reality, but not much. And it's definitely a shock to be reminded how much she has aged since 1996. Dad hangs back and waits for his turn to greet me.

"What's the occasion?" Mum asks.

"I just needed a break from Brisbane," I say vaguely. There will be plenty of time to tell them about Ed later.

"You know you don't need a reason to visit us," Dad says, finally hugging me. "Come in. I've just cooked a crab I caught down at the river."

The mention of seafood triggers off the memory of my dinner with Kurt. Nope. I'm not going to go there.

"Yum. Is there enough to share?"

"Of course."

I dump my bag just inside the door and follow my parents through to the kitchen.

I watch as Mum shuffles over to a big armchair and curls up in it. It's so sad to see that even walking a few feet takes it out of her.

Dad breaks off a claw from the crab and hands it to me with a pair of nutcrackers. I expertly crack the shell and pull the flesh out.

"How've you guys been?" I ask, nibbling the sweet crabmeat.

"So-so," Dad answers for the two of them. "The office has been understaffed lately, so I've been working more hours. Which is good financially, but not so great for your mother."

"It's okay. I've been managing," she says.

"Would it make it easier if I stayed for longer?" I ask.

"No, no. You've got your own life. And also, we don't really have the space for a semi-permanent guest."

"Well, let me know. If it helps, I can come up more often during the week. Just for the day."

"Thanks, honey. We appreciate the offer. Oh, before I forget, your sister's driving up tomorrow, too."

"Really? For how long?"

"She said at least overnight. It's been a while since we've had both daughters under the same roof without partners. I hope you don't mind sharing a room."

"No, I'm fine with it if she is."

While Amy and I haven't been close in recent times, I hope she is as open to a reconciliation as I am.

"Did you want to stay in tonight?" Dad asks. "Or would you like to go out for dinner?"

"It would probably be easier for Mum if we stayed in. I can cook."

"That would be lovely," Mum says. "I've always liked your cooking. I never understood why you gave up such a good job at that restaurant in Brisbane to lock yourself away at home to play on the internet."

The restaurant Mum is talking about was the last place I worked before pursuing my blog full-time. It was a silver service fine dining establishment down on Eagle Street, close to Ed's office. I did enjoy it for a while, and as the executive chef, the money was pretty good—but the hours were horrible, and working in a kitchen during a Brisbane summer was like cooking on the surface of the sun.

I'm about to protest when my mum waves her hand dismissively. "I know, I know. You had your reasons. But then why didn't you go and use that dietician degree or something? They make good money."

"I make good money with my blog, and I get to choose my own hours. You know, Mum, most people are envious of my job."

"I'm proud of you, honey," Dad cuts in. "Your mum's just disappointed she never got to pursue a proper career."

Mum frowns but doesn't correct him.

"What did you want to do?" I ask her. We've never ventured down this path before. I didn't want to upset her when I knew she didn't have the energy to waste.

"I always dreamt of being a dermatologist," she says wistfully.

I blink. "Really?"

"Yes. It pays well and it's meaningful work. But it also requires twelve years of study. Not to mention a body that can move around without getting tired all the time."

"Is there anything else you could do that's similar?" I ask. "Maybe something in alternative medicine that you could pursue at your own pace?"

"I've thought about it. I was actually looking into an acupuncture course recently, but I'm not sure I'm quite up to it right now."

"Well, when you do feel ready, let me know. I'll give you some study tips."

She smiles gratefully before her eyes glaze over. I'm sure I've displayed that expression a lot lately too—a sign of wondering what might have been if life had turned out differently.

"What are you going to make tonight?" Dad asks.

"Um, maybe a cassoulet? I'd probably need to start prepping now, though."

"That sounds delicious."

"All right, I'll see what you have in the cupboard and then I'll do a grocery shop for anything else missing from the recipe."

This is exactly what I needed. Well, not the mini career lecture, but a night with my parents and doing one of my favourite things in the world.

Cooking for people.

***

Dinner is a cruisy affair, made even cruiser by the copious amounts of red wine that Dad keeps pouring into my glass. The cassoulet turned out well, considering I couldn't do the official long-hand version that involves soaking the beans and seasoning the ham hocks and pork shoulder overnight, as well as refrigerating the ragout for an additional twenty-four hours.

It occurs to me that it's strange I married a man who was never home to cook for. And when I think about it, I realise I haven't made a proper dish like this cassoulet for him in months. He didn't seem to appreciate French cooking that much, and opted for Japanese or Mexican when he had the choice. He didn't even really like Italian cooking, except for his beloved mushroom risotto, which I usually saved for birthdays and special occasions.

After dinner, Dad offers to wash up, so I relax in front of the TV with Mum and watch an episode of *Cake Boss*. I love seeing the contestants make those insane gravity-defying structures. I never learned how to do that kind of stuff, because classic French cakes and pastries all have a defined process and look. My job was to just prepare them to the best of my ability, but to be honest, I'm more about the taste than appearances anyway. French onion soup is one of my favourite dishes, but it certainly doesn't look great.

Mum falls asleep less than ten minutes into the show, which leaves Dad and I to chat about what life was like when Amy and I were younger.

"What's your favourite memory?" I ask him.

"The day your sister was born," he says without hesitation. "I have this vivid image of you sitting on the edge of the hospital bed tucked into one of your mother's arms, and Amy was all wrapped up in a blanket on the other side. I have a photo somewhere, but my favourite moment was when Eve and I shared this look, and we knew our family was perfect and complete."

Tears well in my eyes, but I hold them in. I've done enough crying lately. I need to make sure all my memories are appreciated and looked back on with happiness rather than sadness. Just because the world is different now and I know life didn't turn out the way my younger self expected, it shouldn't taint the original events.

I need to remember that.

***

Amy arrives the next morning around 11am. When she sees I'm here, too, she gives me a half-hearted nod of acknowledgement. We almost never catch up, and while I do look forward to seeing her, she makes it very clear she doesn't feel the same.

To be fair, she doesn't seem overly enthusiastic to see Mum and Dad either, and I wonder why she even bothered to make the drive.

I follow her to the guest room where she dumps her bag.

"Did you hit any traffic on the way up?" I ask to get her talking.

"Not much. Just the usual red lights on the north side." She pulls a packet of potato chips from her bag and opens it. She crams a handful into her mouth and holds out the packet to me. I don't take any.

"And you're going back tomorrow?" I check.

"That's the plan. You?"

"Yeah, I'll probably head home then, too. But we'll see."

"What's the ambulance chaser up to?"

"I wish you wouldn't call him that. He's far from an ambulance chaser, for a start. But to answer your question, he's working."

"He works a lot, doesn't he?" She does air quotes when she says the word *work*.

"Yes, and your point is?" I snap. She's either implying he's having an affair or can't stand the sight of me, both which I take offence to. It doesn't matter that the first thing is almost true.

"Sorry. Someone woke up on the wrong side of the bed this morning."

"Um, so you'd be totally fine with me suggesting your boyfriend was cheating on you?" I challenge.

"Whoa. Who said anything about cheating?"

"You know exactly what you were implying."

She walks off in a huff. "I don't have time for this shit."

"Fine. Walk away, then."

I stay in the bedroom and watch her leave. We couldn't even go two minutes without having an argument. I know a lot of siblings disagree, but I feel like Amy makes things particularly difficult.

The only remotely civil conversations we've had in recent times were when I was back in 1996. I wonder if I made a mistake coming up here. Maybe I should have just stayed home and visited the younger version of my family instead.

It gets me wondering…I'd kind of written off anything that happens in 1996 as pointless because they're standalone moments and no one in my current reality knows they even existed, but they're just as real to me as all my other memories, so why shouldn't they be treasured as well?

Once it's happened, *everything* is just memories, and we all have different interpretations of them.

I'm not sure if that makes reality feel less concrete, or 1996's events more so.

I head into Mum and Dad's bedroom, where Mum is propped up against a bunch of pillows, reading a book. She looks up as I enter. "Amy giving you a hard time again?"

I can't help it. I run over and lie down beside her before bursting into tears. "Yes. And I don't know what I've done to deserve it. She's always such a bitch to me."

Mum strokes my hair and makes soothing noises. "I'm sorry, honey. I think you two are just so different, it's hard to find middle ground. And Amy does have a way of speaking without a filter."

"Well, she should learn how to develop one. I'm surprised she has any friends at all if she talks to them the same way she talks to me."

"I know, sweetie. But you might want to go easy on her. She's had a bit of a tough time lately."

More than going through a marriage break-up? I think cynically. But of course, my family doesn't know about that yet.

"What? She broke a fingernail and couldn't get an appointment at her preferred salon?"

"Actually, she had a miscarriage."

I gape. "Really? How? I didn't even know she was seeing anyone."

"She hasn't fully opened up to us yet, so I don't know all the details. Maybe don't tell her you know. She'll explain in her own time."

I can't believe Amy had a miscarriage. My heart goes out to her.

"I might see if she wants to go to the beach or something."

"Okay. But remember, let her set the pace."

"I will."

I go into the living room and find Amy lying on the couch, staring out the window.

"What do you want?" she grumbles.

"I was thinking of heading down the beach. Do you want to come?"

"Not really."

"But it's such beautiful day. Come on. It's probably too cold to go in the water, but we can lie in the sun?"

She drags herself off the couch. "Fine. As long as it means you'll stop bugging me."

Wow. She really makes it difficult to be nice to her.

"Okay. I'll drive. I'll see you at the car in a few minutes."

She nods.

It would be so easy to escape to 1996 right now, but I know I need to work on a few things here.

I can't live in the past forever.

TWENTY-ONE

I haven't been back to Main Street since my last visit to 1996, so it takes a moment for me to readjust again. This is really messing with my head.

Amy was quiet the whole drive. It's much harder to find a place to park now than it was in the nineties, and I end up having to pay for a spot in an undercover garage.

We tramp along the path and down onto the sand. There aren't that many people in the water, but there are quite a few lying on the beach.

Amy and I find a spot and lay out our towels. I slather my skin with 30+. Amy rolls her eyes.

"You were always such a square."

"I'm sorry if that offends you."

"It's just difficult to live up to the example set by the golden child."

"I was *not* the golden child. For the record, you got away with a lot more than I did."

"That's not what I mean. It's like Mum and Dad gave up on me."

"They didn't! And you've probably forgotten, but they tried to talk me out of going to Paris about a million times. Remember?"

"I haven't forgotten, but they were probably like that because they knew you could be anything you wanted. And then when you did amazing with cooking, they accepted it and started bragging about it to all their friends."

"Well, they definitely don't admire what I do now. You should have heard Mum last night lamenting me quitting my last 'proper' job to 'play on the internet.'"

Amy snorts. "Sorry. I don't mean to laugh, but that's kind of funny."

"And they're going to be even more disappointed when they find out my husband left me to go back to his high school sweetheart."

Amy's mouth drops open. "He fucking what?"

I can't really explain anything in detail, so I shrug. "Apparently, I was always his back-up."

My sister looks outraged on my behalf, which I actually find quite sweet. "You know what? I never thought he was right for you."

I'm about to argue when she cuts me off. "I mean, I always thought you were too good for him. I hated that arrogant, distant attitude he had."

"Probably because he was thinking about *her* the whole time," I say gloomily.

"So, when did this all happen?"

"Just in the last few weeks."

"And what? It's all over now? You're getting a divorce?"

"Probably."

She shakes her head. "That's shit." She focuses on me. "You can do so much better. I promise."

"Why are you being nice all of a sudden?"

She doesn't say anything for a moment. I watch her face, and it seems to reflect a sense of regret. But maybe I'm just reading too much into it.

"Well, I never hated you or anything. As I said, it's just been hard to live up to the expectations you set. But now I see you've had it just as hard."

"Are *you* dating anyone?" I ask lightly.

"Not anymore." She traces a pattern in the sand. "Did Mum tell you what happened?"

"She hinted at it," I say, not wanting to admit how much I know.

She sighs. "So, basically we were in love, I got pregnant, I lost the baby at fifteen weeks, and now we can't stand the sight of each other."

I rub her arm. "I'm so sorry."

"It is what it is."

We both look out at the ocean as the waves break gently on the sand.

"How come you never had kids?" she asks.

"I never wanted them," I say automatically.

"See, I'm not sure I believe that. You always talked about having children when you were younger. It wasn't until you married Ed that he brainwashed you into believing you didn't want them either."

"I don't know if that's true, but the thought has crossed my mind recently."

"If Ed called you right now and said he'd made a huge mistake and wanted to start a family, what would you say?"

"I'd say no," I reply firmly. "But only because I don't think I could go back to Ed, regardless of what he said."

"So, you'd consider them with someone else?"

Kurt's face flashes across my mind. No. Just, no.

"I don't know. I'm not sure of anything anymore."

"Well, I hope you meet someone else and manage to have children if that's what you want. You know Brigitte Nielsen had a baby at fifty-four?"

"I'm not even forty, so I won't worry too much about my biological clock just yet."

She's quiet again for a moment, smoothing out the pattern she'd drawn.

"Sorry I was a bitch to you," she says finally.

"That's okay. Sorry I didn't understand where you were coming from."

"Families can be complicated, huh?"

"Yup. So, are you looking for a new partner?"

"I'm taking a break. You?"

"Yeah. I'm taking a break, too."

Amy rubs her hands together to brush off the sand. "You want to get some gelato?"

"Actually, that sounds great."

We leave our towels on the beach and head up to the same gelato shop we've been visiting since we were kids.

It's nice that some things never change.

***

The rest of the day is low key. Amy and I head home after lying in the sun for another hour—and while we don't spend any more time hanging out, when we do pass each other in the hall, it feels relaxed and friendly. Probably more than any other time in our lives.

In the evening while everyone else is watching TV, I lock myself in the guest room and get out my phone. I need to find out where Ed's at, and it's clear he's not going to make the first move. Again. It's been a week since I mentioned we should see lawyers, and while I haven't been able to bring myself to do that yet, I know I'll have to soon.

I shakily dial his number. I don't know why I'm so nervous.

He answers on the first ring. "Hi, Anna?"

"Hey."

"How are you?"

"Good. Can you talk for a minute? You're not working or anything?"

"No, no. I've actually taken a couple of weeks off."

"Oh. Nice." I suddenly feel a little put out. Ed *never* took time off unless it was scheduled months in advance and dedicated to an official holiday outside of Brisbane.

"How have you been?" he asks.

"Um, okay. I'm staying at Mum and Dad's for the weekend."

"That sounds relaxing. Say hi to them for me."

"I will."

"So, was there anything you wanted to talk about in particular?"

"I guess I just wanted to see if you'd contacted a lawyer or anything…"

"Actually, I did. I called one on Monday and I met with him on Wednesday. He seems to think everything will be straightforward if we split our assets down the middle."

I blink. He certainly moved fast. "Great."

"You're happy to sell the house?"

I wouldn't exactly say *happy*…

"Yeah, that's fine. You want me to call an agent?"

"No need. I know a guy who can sort it for us."

"Oh. Cool."

"He can have the photographer out next week and then put up a listing by Friday."

"That soon?"

"He's very efficient."

"It sounds it."

I hear a muffled voice in the background.

"Just a second," Ed calls out.

"Do you have to go?" I ask.

"In a minute. So, we're all good here?"

Is he serious? That's it? Damn it. I can't act like this is purely a business transaction.

"You know what, Ed? No, we're not all good. I know I put this whole thing in motion, but you've just run with it and given almost no regard to my feelings. I'm trying really fucking hard to be mature about it, but it's not easy to just switch off the feelings I've had for you since I was twenty-two. And I'm starting to think those feelings were never reciprocated, or you wouldn't have been able to move on so easily!"

I feel tears rolling down my cheeks. Ed doesn't say anything at first.

"Right," he says after almost a minute. "What do you want me to do?"

"Agh! You're so infuriating! I can't bloody tell you what to do. Just be a fucking empathetic human! Or better yet, think about how you'd react if Maddie was upset. Would you stay silent? Or would you actually use some common decency to try and make her feel better?"

I don't wait for a reply. "I can't do this." I hang up the phone and burst into noisy sobs.

If I had any lingering doubts about ending my marriage before that conversation, they are certainly gone now.

TWENTY-TWO

I sleep badly again, and when I finally get out of bed, a feeling of uneasiness settles over me. I know I was probably a bit harsh on Ed last night, but he was so frustrating. Amy was right. He did always have that distant, arrogant attitude. Like he was above everyone and everything. Including his wife.

Amy heads out early to catch up with an old friend, so I laze around the house for a couple of hours before going for a walk in the national park. At least the weather has been in my favour, with blue sky and sun both days.

I drive down past Main Street and around the point, parking at the edge of the walking path.

I never appreciated this place enough when I lived here. This park is beautiful, with glimpses of the ocean through the pandanus palms at every turn, and the turquoise water changing to ink as you get further away from the bay.

The path is a little crowded, but I shut everyone else out. I spot a couple of whales out near the horizon and the sight momentarily halts the cycle of self-pity running around in my brain.

I find a good vantage point and sit near the edge of a cliff to watch them better.

Damn it. My life is a mess. I no longer feel like I belong in my own time, but I certainly don't belong in 1996 either. Especially when there's no continuity.

I don't know if it's just my mood, but apart from the obvious issue of my marriage, I'm finding the rest of reality more and more unsatisfactory, too. There are so many things I hate about modern life. The way everyone lives on their phones, checking Facebook and uploading their entire existence to Instagram. The way there is no mystery as to the workings of someone's brain…you can read it all online. I don't think I would have been friends with half the people I knew in the nineties if I had understood their true thoughts.

I look down at the phone in my hands, tempted to hurl it off the cliff in front of me. But instead, I sigh and become a hypocrite, searching for distraction online.

I idly scroll through Facebook and read everyone's feeds. I haven't posted in ages, because I don't have anything positive to say, and I've never been one for airing my dirty laundry online.

I hit the search button by accident and see Kelsey's name from last time. I click on her profile and again see her smiling face.

Screw it. I'm contacting her.

Hey, you. I know this might seem out of the blue, but I just wanted to say hi. I know we parted on bad terms, but I want to apologise for how everything went down all those years ago. I was mad because you didn't believe me when I said I didn't sleep with that guy you were dating, but I've missed you so much. I want to resolve this. Can we talk?

A little notification appears to show she's already seen my message. Wow. I kind of wasn't expecting that. I watch as the little dialogue bubbles appear while she replies. I sit there anxiously, waiting to see how she'll respond. I hope she doesn't swear at me. I don't know if I could take it with my current state of mind. Actually, I don't know what I was thinking, contacting her without being properly mentally prepared. I almost switch off the phone, but a message comes through.

I've missed you, too. I know you didn't sleep with Chad. Rachel told me a couple of years later when I saw her—but by then, I thought it was too late and I was scared to get in touch. How are you?

Happy tears well in my eyes.

Me: *I'm all right. Better now I know you're not mad anymore.*

Kelsey: *Where are you?*

Me: *Staying at Mum and Dad's place in Shell Beach.*

Kelsey: *Really? I'm back at Mum's, too! Are you telling me you're only ten minutes away?*

Me: *Yes! I didn't know you were back in town!*

Kelsey: *Long story, but I can explain if you have time. You want to meet at Beans?*

Me: *Sure. When?*

Kelsey: *Now?*

Me: *haha – OK. I'll see you in 15 minutes!*

I love that Kelsey wants us to meet at Beans. It just seems fitting.

I jog all the way back along the path to my car. I wish I had time to change and clean up my face a little, but I'm sure Kelsey will understand I look crap for a reason. And if she's back at her mum's house, there's a chance she won't be looking her best either.

I reach Beans right on time and see Kelsey immediately. She's wearing a pair of black skinny jeans and a paisley top. She has her face buried in her phone, but as soon as she sees me, she jumps up and runs over for a hug.

"Anna!"

"Hey."

She holds me at arm's length and inspects my face. "You look just as pretty as when I last saw you."

"Aw, thanks. That's saying a lot, considering how bad I'm feeling right now."

"Ugh, don't worry. Look at this," she says, indicating her own face. She actually looks really good. Much better than me at the moment. Her hair has been freshly coloured and styled, and her face is made up subtly with some bronzer on her cheeks and a pale pink lip gloss.

"You look great. Have you ordered anything yet?"

"No, I was waiting for you. But I'm actually kind of hungry. Are you ready for lunch?"

"Oh, yeah. I could eat." Kelsey hands me the menu from her table and I quickly scan it. "I think I'll have a BLT."

"Great idea. I'll have one of those, too. And an orange juice."

"Let's go order together and then we can catch up."

We both pay our own way and sit back down at the table.

Kelsey stares at me. "I can't believe it's taken us this long to catch up again. Was it really around 2000 when we last hung out?"

My last conversation with sixteen-year-old Kelsey was only a few weeks ago. I want to so badly tell her what I've gone through, but I know she won't believe me. I could always try the Mr. Green reference, but I'm not sure that would be a good idea so soon after reconnecting.

"It doesn't seem that long," I say, compromising.

"I know. I can't believe I trusted that jackass over you. I'm sure a tiny part of me knew you didn't really sleep with him, but he said he knew about that little heart-shaped birthmark on your butt."

I slap her arm playfully. "*Everybody* knew about that birthmark, remember? We went out one night and got really drunk and you started telling everyone."

"I don't remember that."

"Well, you did."

"God, I'm sorry. I hope we can be friends again. No one gets me like you used to."

"I hope I don't disappoint you now."

"I'm sure you won't."

"So, what's been happening?"

Her face falls. "Well, Andy's finally out of jail. I'm guessing you heard about everything that happened?"

"Sort of."

"I won't go into the details now, but it wasn't pretty. He's staying at Mum's, too, and it makes me uncomfortable. I'm going to have to find my own place again soon."

"Where were you living before that?"

"I was in Buderim with my husband, Aaron."

"Don't tell me…"

She nods grimly. "Yep. Aaron from high school. The one I could never get interested in me when we were sixteen. We reconnected in 2014 when I was visiting Mum one weekend, and we ran into each other at the supermarket. He wasn't as hot as when we were at school, but he was so nice to me. He'd gone through a pretty rough decade and seemed humbled by it all. He asked me out for a drink, and I guess I kind of felt sorry for him. Plus, I felt like I owed it to my teenage self to give him a chance."

I laugh. "You're a crack-up."

"I don't know what happened, but we sort of just fell into a relationship. He made all the effort. and I went along with it. But I sort of knew right from the beginning it was a mistake."

I ignore the similarities between Kelsey and Aaron's relationship with mine and Ed's for the moment because I was basically in Aaron's role. "But you still married him?"

"Yeah," she sighs. "It was kind of a spur of the moment thing. We were on a holiday in the US, and I was using the trip to kind of decide whether to persevere when we got home. And then one night in Vegas we were both really drunk and ended up getting hitched at one of those awful Elvis chapels. I regretted it the next morning."

"Oh no. A bit of a cliché, huh?"

"Tell me about it. And you know what? Some of those Elvis chapels are really gross. They're outside the main strip and they're really grungy and depressing."

"So, what happened after that?"

"Well, until that point, I had actually been planning to leave him as soon as we got home, but then I couldn't. He was so excited and totally oblivious to my misery."

"How long did you last?"

"A year. But you know what the final straw was?"

"What?"

"We were at his parents' house one afternoon and everyone was sitting around watching the football on TV, and I made some comment about reading an article on the gender pay gap. Aaron turned to me and said, 'Oh God, Kelsey, you're not one of those crazy feminists, are you?'"

I roar with laughter. I knew even back in high school how strong and pro-women's rights Kelsey was. I can only imagine her position would have solidified over time.

"And so you just walked out?"

"Pretty much. I moved in with a friend for a while, but she lost her job, and I couldn't afford to pay the rent on my own, so I ended up going back to Mum's. I swear it was the most depressing day of my life when I pulled up in her driveway with all my stuff, divorced and single again."

"I know exactly what you mean," I say, sighing.

Kelsey looks at me, surprised. "You're divorced, too?"

"I will be soon."

"Oh, I'm so sorry. That sucks, Anna. But if I'm being honest, I'm kind of glad. Now I don't feel so alone."

"If my misfortune helps anyone in any way, I'm happy," I say.

Our food arrives and we eat quietly. My personal life might be pretty miserable right now, but at least I have Kelsey back in it.

TWENTY-THREE

After lunch, Kelsey tells me she has to take her mother to a doctor's appointment, but she would like to meet up again later for drinks. I like that it gives me something to focus on for the rest of the day, instead of dwelling on how crappy things are with Ed.

Yet again, he hasn't tried to get in touch. Surely if you knew your wife was upset, you'd check on her.

It's not like I even want us to get back together anymore. I just want to know that he cares about me as a person. That all those years we spent together meant something to him, even if it wasn't 'true love.'

I spend a little time in the afternoon catching up on some admin, and then take a leisurely bath before properly doing myself up. Nothing extravagant, just styling my hair—this time with a proper hair straightener—and putting on some makeup.

I hadn't realised, but in the last few weeks, I haven't had much of an appetite, so my outfits are a little looser on my body. That has never happened in the past. Normally, I put on weight when I'm depressed. This break-up has really affected me.

I go downstairs, and Dad does that cheesy thing dads do and whistles at my appearance.

"You look great, honey."

"Thanks, Dad," I say, embarrassed.

"Where are you off to?" he asks.

"Just out for drinks with Kelsey."

"Do you want a lift?"

"Actually, that would be nice. Thanks. I don't plan on drinking too much, but just in case."

"Are you ready to go now?"

"If you are."

"I'll just grab my keys."

I wave goodbye to Mum, who is on the couch as usual. It must be so hard being a spectator to everyone else's life and not having your own. I hope medicine progresses enough to help her out sooner rather than later.

"How's Mum doing, mentally?" I ask Dad once we're in the car.

"She has her moments. Some days are harder than others."

"How are you coping?"

"The same. It's hard seeing someone you love suffer."

"I know."

"That extends to you and Amy as well. All my girls are going through a hard time at the moment, but you're the only one who hasn't told me why."

I tear up. I didn't really want to get into it with Mum or Dad this weekend, but I suppose there's no point putting it off any longer.

"Ed and I have separated."

He nods. "I'm not surprised."

I stare at him. "I am!"

"Surely you knew deep down he wasn't the person you'd spend the rest of your life with?"

"Actually, yes, I did think I would spend the rest of my life with him. I wouldn't have married him otherwise." I don't want to admit the thoughts I've had since, which question the level of delusion I experienced to make me feel that way.

"I always thought you'd end up with someone a little less serious. You always had such a zest for life. And then when you met Ed, you seemed to adopt his personality. It made me sad to see the little girl I used to know disappear."

"How come you've never mentioned any of this before?"

"Because it wouldn't have done any good. It's my job to support you, no matter the decisions you make. Was it your choice to separate?"

"Sort of."

"How are you feeling about it? I mean, apart from the obvious?"

"I think it's too early to say. But I'm hopeful there will be a day sometime in the future when life feels normal again."

"Good. That's all I needed to hear. I know your mother said there wasn't enough space at the apartment for a semi-permanent guest, but she just didn't want to be a burden on you. If you need somewhere to stay, you're more than welcome to spend as much time as you need with us."

I brush a stray tear from my cheek. "Thanks, Dad. I'll keep that in mind."

We reach Main Street, and I pause to wrap him up in a tight hug. "I love you," I whisper.

"I love you, too, honey. Will you catch a cab home later?"

"Either that or an Uber. But there's a chance I might go back to Kelsey's, too." Once I turned eighteen, Mum and Dad said if I couldn't get home by midnight, then they'd prefer I stayed at a friend's house to avoid waking them up.

Dad laughs. "You're welcome to return after midnight if that's what you're worried about."

"Either way, I'll figure something out." I give him a last peck on the cheek and jump out of the car.

Kelsey told me to meet her down the end of Main Street at a new place she discovered. When I enter the bar, I see her and another woman sitting at a nearby counter. They have their backs to me, so I can't tell who the other person is. I'm sort of annoyed Kelsey didn't warn me she'd be bringing someone. I'm not in the mood to be the odd one out if she's her new bestie or anything.

"Hey, guys," I say cautiously.

Kelsey spins around, beaming. "Hey! You look awesome! And look who I found! I thought I'd see if anyone from the old gang was still in town."

The other woman faces me with a genuine smile. "Anna! Hey!"

"Rachel! Oh my God! It's been, what, like, twenty years?"

"I know. Wow, you haven't changed a bit."

"You either. Well, except for the hair. But I really like this look on you."

Rachel used to have long dark hair, but now it's cropped into a cute bob and dyed a golden blonde.

"Thanks!"

The initial shock of seeing her wears off, and I suddenly realise something.

Rachel is Kurt's cousin.

My heart starts hammering.

"Anna is just about to join the divorce club, too," Kelsey explains.

"Ugh, I'm sorry to hear that," Rachel says. "I split up with my second husband last year."

I blink. "You've been married *twice*?"

"Yup. I should have learned after the first time, but apparently not." She laughs and picks up the glass in front of her, taking a large gulp.

"Guys suck," Kelsey says. She pats the stool next to her. "Sit down and grab a drink," she instructs.

I oblige and order myself a passionfruit mojito. I need to grill Rachel about Kurt. Or do I? Now probably isn't the right time.

"So, you never left Shell Beach?" I ask instead.

"Nope. I'm glad, too. It's such a beautiful town. And everyone who left comes back eventually. Look at you two!"

"Actually, I'm only up for the weekend," I clarify. "But I do plan on visiting more often."

"Good. It's a shame we all lost touch for so long, huh? I think the friends you make at school are the ones who understand you the best. I've made some other friends over the years, but it's not quite the same. Oh, Anna, Kelsey mentioned you live in Brisbane, so I should put you in touch with Jackson. You remember he used to work at Beans? He's been living down there for ages."

"Oh, I would love to see Jackson! I was just thinking about him the other day!"

And talking to him, but I can't tell them that.

"Remind me to give you his number later."

"I will."

My mojito arrives, and I take a sip. Yum. "This is a cool place," I say to Kelsey.

"I know. I don't mind how they've prettied up Main Street over the last twenty years. Mind you, I still have fond memories of the nineties. We practically lived at Beans, didn't we?"

"I think I still prefer Beans," I say. "But I'm open to new things as well." I turn to Rachel. "What's your brother up to these days?"

"Oh, Chris. He's a big disappointment to my parents," she laughs. "Instead of going to uni, he went overseas and became a scuba diving instructor. He's based in Koh Samui right now."

"That sounds like fun. Have you been to visit him?"

"Once. I've been meaning to book another trip, actually."

I'm trying to formulate a way to naturally divert the conversation to her cousin when Kelsey cuts in. "Well, he's a lot less of a disappointment than my brother."

"Yeah, I was sorry to hear about Andy," Rachel says. "I always thought he was a little…"

"Psychotic?" Kelsey provides.

"Um, possibly?" Rachel says awkwardly.

"Don't worry. I always knew he had problems. I just didn't realise how big they were until he was caught."

"You can't help who you're related to," I say gently.

"You're right. Speaking of family, how's that sister of yours?"

"Normally, I'd say I have no idea, but we kind of did the whole sibling bonding thing yesterday and it was nice."

"Well, the men we thought we could count on might have let us down, but at least we have each other."

"That's right." Rachel picks up her glass and clinks it with each of ours.

"Cheers to being friends forever."

***

For the next couple of hours, we get increasingly drunk. The bar also serves food, so we make our way over to a booth and order a couple of pizzas.

I still haven't found a way to ask Rachel about Kurt, but I know my window of opportunity is closing as the night wears on.

And then I think of the perfect segue.

"I found my old diaries the other day," I tell the girls. "And I was reading about how we used to go down to The Palace, but sometimes we'd go across the street to that old record shop. I miss record shops."

"And video stores," Kelsey adds.

Rachel nods in an exaggerated fashion, thanks to the alcohol in her bloodstream. "Me, too. Hey, my cousin used to work at that record shop."

And there it is. Even though I expected him to exist in reality, hearing it from Rachel's mouth makes it properly official.

"How come we never talked to him when we went there?" I ask.

"Actually, I don't know. I guess he was only there for a year, and maybe he wasn't working on the days we visited. I'm sure I would have told you, though."

It's possible. My sixteen-year-old self would not have remembered Rachel vaguely commenting on how a cousin I never met worked there.

"Why was he only there for a year?" I ask. I know that's kind of a weird question to ask, but Rachel doesn't seem to notice. I'm grateful I can use the cover of drunkenness to excuse anything odd I say.

"Oh, he was studying music production or something. He ended up moving to London and becoming a fancy music producer."

Butterflies swarm in my belly. He might still be the same person I met in 1996!

"Is he still there? Would I have heard of any of his music?"

"Uh, yeah, last I heard he was still there. He works with a lot of famous DJs, apparently. We never really talked in the end, because Dad didn't like how he was a bad influence on me and Chris." She giggles. "If only he knew what Chris and I got up to even without Kurt."

I feel the moment slipping away. Quick. What can I ask?

"So, Chris doesn't see him either?"

"He might have visited him once." She squints as if trying to think hard. "Oh, that's right. They caught up in Paris, and Chris mentioned how he was intimidated by Kurt and his model girlfriend..." She narrows her eyes at me. "Hang on, why are you asking all these questions about my cousin?"

"No reason," I say, a sick feeling settling in my chest. Of course he would have a girlfriend. And a model one at that.

Kelsey looks at me strangely. "Are you okay?"

"Yeah, I'm fine. Sorry. I think I've had too much to drink. My brain was doing that thing where you keep asking questions but don't have any idea why."

"Is that a thing?" Rachel asks, laughing.

"Yeah, I can relate," Kelsey says after a second. "But you know what the cure for that is?"

"What?" I ask.

"Shots!"

I try to protest, but Kelsey insists. She orders some tequila shots, followed by a round of B52s.

After that, I feel very much like I do just after taking the youth compound.

I think I might be about to black out.

TWENTY-FOUR

When I first wake up the next morning, I worry that I actually *did* take some of the youth compound and ended up back in 1996.

I'm disoriented for a moment, and when I look around, I see I'm in Kelsey's bedroom. How did *that* happen?

But when I focus on the walls, I see that they no longer feature movie posters. Instead, they are adorned with eclectic art. There are no CDs on the floor, and the furniture is slightly more modern.

I roll over and look at the person next to me. I let out a sigh of relief when I see that it's Kelsey, but very much the almost-forty version.

Why am I here?

Oh, that's right. The shots.

And Rachel.

And learning that Kurt is alive, but he's a bigshot music producer in London and has a model girlfriend.

I almost wish I *were* back in 1996. At least I know that Kurt is single then. At least, I assume he is.

My phone beeps. Kelsey groans.

"It's too early for noise," she says, burying her head under her pillow. I smile despite my hangover. She said something similar the last time I woke up here.

"Sorry," I whisper as I roll out of bed. I grab my phone and head downstairs.

I freeze when I see Andy watching TV, but he doesn't seem to notice me. Good.

I sit outside on the driveway and wait for a small wave of nausea to subside before looking at the message on my phone. It's from Ed.

I suddenly feel guilty. Here I've been mad at him, when I spent the evening pining after another guy. I'm as bad as he is.

I read the message.

Are you still up the coast? Is it OK if I drop by the house and pick up some of my stuff?

Really? He's that eager to avoid me that he times a visit when he knows I won't be at home?

That's fine. I'll still be here for a few more hours.

Thanks. Talk again soon.

Talk again soon? Could he be any more impersonal?

For the second time in two days, I feel like throwing my phone away.

I notice I have one more message.

This is Rachel! Also, call Jackson! His number is 0482 654 103.

I smile, saving both Rachel and Jackson's numbers to my contacts. It will be nice to see Jackson again.

I head back inside.

"Anna. You didn't say hello before. That's very rude, you know."

I look at Andy as I continue walking up the stairs. "Sorry. Hello."

He looks like he's contemplating whether to harass me further but decides I'm not worth the trouble.

He looks back at the TV.

I like to think I could fight him off if he tried anything, but the truth is, I still find him quite unnerving. I just hope he's learned something from his time in jail.

I obviously didn't bring a change of clothes with me last night, so I pick up my handbag and lean down to whisper in Kelsey's ear.

"I'm going home now. I'll call you later and we'll arrange another catch-up."

She murmurs something that sounds like "talk soon, babe," and rolls over.

I head back out and realise I'm in the same position I was back in 1996 without a car.

At least I can afford a cab this time.

***

Back at Mum and Dad's, I tidy up and pack my things. Amy returned to Brisbane last night, but she left a message with Dad saying she'd call me next week. The idea of meeting up with my sister for a girls' lunch sometime in the near future makes me happy.

I give Mum a big hug. "If you're feeling up to it, I'd like you and Dad to come stay with me sometime soon."

"We would love that, honey. I'll let you know."

I'm starting to appreciate family and old friends a lot more than I used to.

I drive home, stopping at Chermside along the way to grab some lunch and do a little shopping. It was obvious Ed didn't want to see me, and my hangover has made me want to avoid loud noises—which might happen in the form of yelling if I see my almost ex-husband today.

I get home around 3pm and notice the rest of his clothes are gone. I wonder if he's living with Maddie now. He's also taken a selection of our furnishings, including a couple of paintings and some of the kitchen stuff. I don't really care, though. Ed can have all that crap. Once we sell the house, I'll probably want to buy new stuff anyway. Get a fresh start.

I spend the rest of the afternoon working on a new recipe, this time just a couple of smoothies I recommend for people when they're trying to avoid overdosing on winter comfort food.

Before I left, I had tucked the youth compound in the back of the bathroom cabinet behind a jewellery box. I think it's best if it stays there for now. By revisiting 1996, I'm just making it harder to move on in the present. I need to stay with these uncomfortable feelings and face them head on. The past isn't going anywhere, and I know I'll be able to access it again if and when I need to.

But for now, I need to look forward.

THREE MONTHS LATER…

"Thank you so much for coming down and helping me pack," I say to Kelsey as I let her into the house.

She steps inside and looks around as I lead her towards the living room.

"No problem. I must say, your house is lovely, but it's not the kind of style I would have picked for you."

"Why not?"

"I don't know. It's just so sterile. You used to love colour in everything."

"Yeah, but that was the nineties. Everyone loved colour then."

"I don't know. I feel like you'd be more suited to an eclectic style. It would fit better with your creative personality."

I never really thought about it, but she might be right. Ed and I spent so much time curating our image that we kind of forgot to put any life into it. Which probably says a lot about why our marriage failed.

"Hmm, maybe," I say noncommittally. "Hey, would you like a drink? Just put your bag in the spare room." I point down the hall.

She heads towards the spare room and calls back over her shoulder. "Is it too early for wine?"

"It's never too early for wine." Even though it *is* only 2pm.

I pour a couple of glasses of Prosecco and hand her one when she reappears. She takes a sip and surveys the room. "You have a lot of stuff."

"I know. I never realised. And it's all useless junk. I'm thinking of offering half of it to Ed or donating it to charity."

"Sounds like a plan. How about we make one pile over near the door with anything you want to get rid of, and then we'll pack the rest?"

"Okay."

"Sorry I haven't come down earlier to visit. Work has been insane! We seem to have a function for two hundred people every weekend! I swear I've done eighty hours a week for the last two months."

Since Kelsey and I reconciled, I've learnt that she gave up teaching a while back and went into event planning instead. Apparently organising peoples' wedding receptions is less stressful than looking after a bunch of kids. She currently manages functions at an upmarket golf club on the outskirts of Shell Beach.

"That's all right. I've been busy sorting out all the legal stuff. At least Ed hasn't made things difficult."

"Why would he? He's the one with the new partner."

"I know. But I've heard so many horror stories from people who divorce, and everyone gets so bitter and evil."

"It wasn't really like that with me and Aaron. But then he was pretty clueless about everything. He was happy for me to take care of all the paperwork."

"I guess we're both sort of lucky in that regard."

"Ha. Yeah. Anyway, where do you want me to start? In here? The bedroom? The bathroom?"

"Actually, the bathroom will probably be easiest. Just put everything in a box and I'll go through what I want to throw away later."

"Sure."

"I'll do the bedroom so we can still talk through the doorway."

"Sweet."

We head to our respective posts, and I start folding clothes from my drawers into a box. I hear Kelsey shuffling around in the bathroom.

"I think we should go out tonight," she calls out.

"What did you have in mind?"

"Nothing too over the top. Maybe just dinner and a few drinks somewhere?"

"I guess we could go to Cloudland? They have this amazing mushroom and truffle pizza…"

"You had me at pizza. And doubly at truffles."

I laugh. "Cool."

"Hey, speaking of food, I have a proposition for you."

"Do you now?"

"I do. So, you know how I'm a well-respected and experienced event planner with glittering references, and you're a famous food blogger?"

"Yes…"

"Well, I think we should go into business together."

I stop and go stand in the doorway to stare at her. "You're serious?"

"Yes, why? You don't think it's a good idea?"

"Actually, I really like the idea. But do you think it will work? And we won't kill each other?"

"All I can say is that I'll try really hard not to kill you, but I *do* think it would work. We know each other so well that we don't have to worry about figuring out whether our personalities would clash. And besides, it would be an equal partnership with me out the front and you out the back. During work hours, we wouldn't actually have much time to talk to each other."

A tiny seed of excitement blooms in my belly. I really like this idea. I need something new to focus on, and lately my blog has not been enough of a distraction.

"What kind of business did you have in mind?"

"Do you want me to pitch you my concept right now?"

"Do you have a concept to pitch to me right now?"

"I do."

"Then go ahead."

"Okay, well, I didn't think I'd be doing it from inside your bathroom, but here goes. It would be a dessert restaurant and we'd call it Naughty or Nice. Half the dishes would be your fancy authentic French stuff, and the other half would be the kind of recipes you put on your blog."

I feel a huge grin forming on my face. "And we could furnish half of it in pink and half in black!"

"See, I knew you were secretly a colour fiend. Yes! It's perfect. What do you say?"

"I say, I love it! But we'll need to do a lot of preparation first. And figure out where we're going to get the money from." I stop. "Hang on, where are we going to open this place?"

"I was thinking probably down here in Brisbane. It would be riskier opening at Shell Beach, and we can't really afford the rent on Main Street."

"So, you'd move down here?"

"I would. But don't worry, I wouldn't ask to live with you. I think that would be pushing our luck a little too far. However, I talked to Jackson the other day and he's looking for a roommate. I could maybe live with him."

I clap my hands together. "This is so exciting! I definitely want to explore this further. And actually, I had heard that Jackson was looking for someone, so that would be handy."

Right after that weekend at Mum and Dad's, I'd phoned Jackson, and we'd met for coffee. He's now one of my besties (apart from Kelsey, of course) and I definitely wouldn't have coped as well during the last few months of my marriage break-up without having him to rely on.

"We could invite him to Cloudland tonight, too, and ask him," Kelsey suggests.

"That's a great idea. Kelsey, you're amazing, you know that?"

"I do my best," she says with fake modesty.

I return to putting clothes in boxes, and Kelsey continues packing my bathroom stuff.

"You have a lot of crap in your cupboards," she says. "I'm going to need two boxes."

"That's fine. As I said, I'll sort out everything later. But maybe put the stuff you know I'll use right away in one and the rest in the other."

"Will do."

I smile to myself as I look around my bedroom. I'm glad I'm moving on. Ed and I have met up a couple of times in the last few months, but it was mostly to discuss logistics about our future. I was surprised to find I harboured no further resentment towards him during our last get-together, and I hope that one day we can maybe be friends again. I think that will be easy, considering our relationship was more platonic than romantic even while we were married.

I haven't talked to Maddie since that time we met at Jocelyn's, and she hasn't tried to contact me either. I think that's for the best. Perhaps one day in the future, I'll be able to talk to her again, too.

But the thing that makes me sadder than the end of my marriage is knowing that Kurt is out there somewhere, with someone else. We never even stood a chance in the real world.

But like Grandma Millie, I'm definitely a believer in more than one soulmate, so I'm hopeful someone just as perfect as Kurt will come along eventually.

Kelsey lugs two boxes through the doorway and drops them at my feet.

"Done."

I look down, knowing the youth compound is inside one of them.

And I guess if I don't find someone else, I can always go back to 1996.

In the meantime, I have a life to live.

Right now.

Thanks for reading *1996!*

I really hope you enjoyed it. If you'd like to get in touch, I can be found on most social media and book-related websites. Reviews on your preferred platform are always appreciated, as are personal messages.

Also, if you'd like a FREE copy of *Before Coco Bay*, sign up to my newsletter at https://www.kirstymcmanus.com.au/get-free-stuff/

Read on for a sample of *1997* and a list of my other books.

Kirsty.

Facebook: /kirstymcmanusauthor
Instagram: /kirstymcauthor
Goodreads:
https://www.goodreads.com/author/show/5434523.Kirsty_McManus
Amazon: https://www.amazon.com/Kirsty-McManus/e/B006QCN6AW
Bookbub: @KirstyMcManus
Web: https://kirstymcmanus.com.au

ONE

It's been seven months since my life changed forever. Seven months since I burst out of *The Matrix* after living for years and years in total blissful ignorance. Until that point, I thought my life was perfect. I had a handsome husband, a beautiful house, and a great job.

And then BLAM!

A weird psychedelic drug thrust me back into 1996, and I discovered that my husband never loved me as much as he loved someone else.

It came as quite a shock.

Since then, I've been finding it a bit difficult to come to terms with my new reality. Mind you, it hasn't been all bad. I've reconnected with a bunch of old friends, and my relationship with my sister is stronger than ever— but to adjust to being single after an eighteen-year relationship is definitely not what I'd call easy.

"Anna?"

I look up. Kelsey is staring at me.

"Sorry, what?"

"You're off in la-la land again, aren't you?"

"I'm trying really hard not to be."

She sighs. "Well, how about we call it a day and then meet again on Monday? We still have a lot to do."

"I know. Thank you for being so understanding. I'm sorry I'm distracted."

Since Kelsey and I reconciled, we've decided to go into business together. She'd been an event planner at a Shell Beach golf club for a few years but was wanting to go out on her own at some point—and because she knew I was a pastry chef and healthy dessert creator, she thought we'd make the perfect partnership. We are currently in my kitchen discussing our new venture's progress, a sort-of concept café called Naughty or Nice.

"Next week, we need to finalise the menu so we can send it off to the printers. And the builders called this morning to say most of the fit-out will be complete in a couple of days. Have you spoken to Amy?"

My sister offered us her interior design skills to make sure that what we envisioned in our heads looked the same in real life. Initially, I was worried we might not work well together, considering I was basically estranged from her for twenty years, but it's been really easy. And fun. She definitely deserves her reputation as one of the city's best designers. Plus, she's not even charging me for her time, which is a huge bonus.

"I spoke to her yesterday. She's just waiting on a friend of hers to finish constructing the chandelier."

The centrepiece of our whole shop is going to be a massive cascade of bubble-shaped lights hanging at the back of the store.

"Cool. And how are you going with—"

My phone cuts off Kelsey's next question. It's Rachel. Since we reconnected last year, she's also become one of my best friends, but she still lives up at Shell Beach. She recently mentioned wanting to have a weekend in Brisbane, so I've invited her to stay.

Kelsey rolls her eyes. "Go on. Answer it."

I mouth her a *thank you* and pick up my phone.

"Hey!" The sound is slightly muffled, so I assume Rachel is in her car. "I'm about fifteen minutes away. Are you at home?"

"I am. Kelsey and I are just finishing up a business meeting."

"Great! See you soon!"

I hang up and look at Kelsey. "Rachel's almost here, so it's probably a good time to wrap this up anyway. Are you sure you can't come out with us tonight?"

"Sorry, no. I have a date."

"With Ben?" Ben is the latest in a string of toy-boys Kelsey has started seeing. She figures it's a win-win situation, because she doesn't want to settle down with anyone, and they don't usually want to, either. I envy her confidence. I would struggle to get naked in front of a man more than five years my junior.

"Yep."

"That must be getting dangerously close to a serious relationship," I tease.

"I wouldn't call three dates serious. But I do like him. And that body!" She fans herself in an exaggerated fashion.

"Okay, okay. I don't want to know. See you next week?"

"Yes! Have fun with Rachel tonight! And don't do anything I wouldn't do."

"Which is what, exactly?"

"I wouldn't go home alone," she says, eyes twinkling.

I shoot her a look. "Kelsey…"

Kelsey thinks my life would be perfect if only I had someone new in it. But I am definitely not ready for a new relationship. I'm still recovering from a divorce. Not to mention trying to forget a certain other person I met last year.

She holds her hands up in surrender. "What? I'm not hassling you."

"All right." I give her a quick hug and see her out.

I go over to the stereo and choose some old Backstreet Boys tunes to get me in a party mood.

Just as I'm singing along to *Everybody* and getting my nineties dance groove on, my phone rings again.

It's Mum.

"Hey, Mum! How are you?"

"Good. Great, actually. I've been trying a bunch of new strategies in an attempt to treat this damn fatigue, and they're sort of working. Finally."

"Oh, that's amazing! I'm so glad you're feeling better." Mum has been battling myalgic encephalomyelitis, otherwise known as chronic fatigue syndrome, for almost two decades now.

"Thanks, honey. I know it's early days, and I don't expect a miracle cure, but I've actually been able to start doing stuff like walk into town without it wiping me out for the rest of the week."

"Does that mean you might be able to come for a visit soon? Maybe the café opening? We're having a small party on Saturday the twenty-fifth."

"Oh, sweetie, I would love that. I can't promise anything, but I'll do everything in my power to get down there and see you. Amy sent me a couple of photos of the place, and it looks fantastic. I'm so proud of you two girls."

"Thanks, Mum." I start to tear up. I do that a lot lately. I think going through a marriage break-up can make you super emotional, even when stuff unrelated to the break-up happens.

"Anyway, I just wanted to let you know that I've been thinking of you, and I'm looking forward to seeing you again soon."

"I really appreciate it. I'm looking forward to seeing you, too."

I hang up, smiling. Life feels much friendlier these days. Well, apart from my relationship with Ed. And I don't think I could ever be besties with Maddie, even though I'm the one who reintroduced her to my now ex-husband. But I'm grateful for all the other relationships I've re-ignited lately.

I quickly straighten up my apartment in preparation for Rachel's arrival. I currently rent a one-bedroom place on the second floor of an old building in Kangaroo Point. I don't have a view of the river, but I am only a block back from the water.

Just as I'm contemplating getting something to drink, the doorbell rings. I fling open the door and Rachel throws her arms around me.

"It's so good to see you!" she says, obviously very excited about being in the city for the weekend.

I hug her back, laughing. "You, too."

"God, I love Brisbane. I don't know if I could live here full-time, but I certainly appreciate the convenience. Everything in Shell Beach closes at 9pm. I can't believe that's the time we're going to be heading out later!"

"It certainly has its benefits. But then, you do have that gorgeous beach."

"True."

I head through to the kitchen and open the fridge. "Would you like a drink?"

"Yes, please."

I pull out a bottle of Prosecco and pour us two glasses, handing her one.

"To getting back out into the scary social jungle," I say, clinking her drink with mine.

"You're right about the scary part. Even the guys on the coast are hard work. I can't imagine what the city boys are going to be like."

"Well, I'm not planning on meeting anyone tonight. I just want to see what's out there."

"I totally understand. I think even when I meet someone new, I'm going to keep it casual. I like my freedom."

"Me, too. So, we'll be all modern and self-sufficient, just with our hot man on call when we need him?"

She giggles. "Exactly."

We down our drinks, and I let Rachel shower while I get out some crackers and cheese. I refill our glasses and queue a few more nineties songs on the stereo. Except then I start thinking of Kurt—even though I'm pretty sure he would never have listened to Ace of Base or En Vogue.

In this reality, he's taken on the form of a distant celebrity—which I guess he kind of is, producing music for famous DJs in London. I can't even look him up, because he doesn't seem to share the same surname with the cousin currently in my bathroom—and when I googled *Kurt music producer London* there were a lot of results. The ones with photos clearly weren't him, and I wasn't about to start randomly emailing the rest. Besides, what would I say? *Hi, you don't know me, but I've met you multiple times in an alternate reality?*

I also don't want to mess with his life if he's happily settled with someone else. I can't be the Maddie in that relationship.

But I so badly want to ask Rachel if she's heard anything else…maybe that he's broken up with his girlfriend and is moving back to Australia? Except I don't want her thinking I'm only friends with her again so I can grill her about him. In her version of reality, I've never met the guy. I already asked too many questions once, and she started to get suspicious. Luckily, she was drunk and hopefully forgot soon after.

No, the best thing to do is try and move on. Kurt isn't real. At least not the version I met. He's just an echo of the past. Who knows what the current incarnation is like? I almost don't want to know. It might be like that time I met a celebrity chef I was kind of obsessed with and he turned out to be a total dick.

I take a large swallow from my refilled glass and wait for Rachel to reappear.

She soon does, wearing a tight pink dress and tall strappy black heels.

"Wow. You look amazing!"

"Thanks, hon. I feel like I should at least dress like I belong in the city."

"You're definitely going to turn heads tonight." I point to her drink. "I got you another one. And feel free to change the music if you're not into Jamiroquai or The Fugees."

"I love this stuff!" She dances around to prove her point. "Go on, get ready so we can catch up properly."

I obey, heading off to the shower.

I have a good feeling about tonight.

Read the rest here: https://mybook.to/1997

BOOKS BY KIRSTY MCMANUS

My Own Personal Rockstar

https://mybook.to/MyOwnPersonalRockstar

Love at Coco Bay (Coco Bay Series Book #2)

https://mybook.to/LoveAtCocoBay

Welcome to Coco Bay (Coco Bay Series Book #1)

https://mybook.to/WelcomeToCocoBay

Before Coco Bay (A Coco Bay Series prologue)

https://mybook.to/BeforeCocoBay

A Christmas Rescue
(co-authored with Diane Michaels)

https://mybook.to/AChristmasRescue

Mind Reader

https://mybook.to/MindReader

I Thought It Was You

https://mybook.to/IThoughtItWasYou

1998 (90s Flashback Series Book #3)

https://mybook.to/1998

1997 (90s Flashback Series Book #2)

https://mybook.to/1997

1996 (90s Flashback Series Book #1)

https://mybook.to/1996

MultiDate

https://mybook.to/MultiDate

Lightweight

https://mybook.to/Lightweight

Perfume Therapy

https://mybook.to/PerfumeTherapy

How Not To Handle a Breakup

(formerly Saved by the Celebutante)

https://mybook.to/HowNotToHandleABreakup

Zen Queen

https://mybook.to/ZenQueen

ABOUT THE AUTHOR

Kirsty McManus was born in Sydney, Australia and moved to Queensland when she was 14. When she was 25, she lived in Japan for a year with her partner Kesh and worked as an English teacher. This was the inspiration behind her debut novel, *Zen Queen*. She also spent a year in Canada and then settled back down on the Sunshine Coast in 2008. Her writing often features characters visiting different countries and / or finding themselves in unusual situations. She is a little bit obsessed with vampires (Damon and Stefan are her favourites) and hopes to one day write her own epic vampire series.

Made in United States
Troutdale, OR
05/05/2024

19608357R10126